Surviving the Holocaust and Stalin

Surviving the Holocaust and Stalin

The Amazing Story of the Seiler Family

Vanessa Holburn

PEN & SWORD
HISTORY

AN IMPRINT OF PEN & SWORD BOOKS LTD.
YORKSHIRE – PHILADELPHIA

First published in Great Britain in 2023
by Vanessa Holburn
An imprint of
Pen & Sword Books Limited
Yorkshire – Philadelphia

Copyright © Vanessa Holburn, 2023

ISBN 978 1 39906 299 2

Typeset in INDIA by IMPEC eSolutions
Printed and bound in the UK by CPI Group (UK) Ltd, Croydon, CRO 4YY

Pen & Sword Books Limited incorporates the imprints of Atlas, Archaeology,
Aviation, Discovery, Family History, Fiction, History, Maritime, Military,
Military Classics, Politics, Select, Transport, True Crime, Air World,
Frontline Publishing, Leo Cooper, Remember When, Seaforth Publishing,
The Praetorian Press, Wharncliffe Local History, Wharncliffe Transport,
Wharncliffe True Crime and White Owl.

For a complete list of Pen & Sword titles please contact
PEN & SWORD BOOKS LIMITED
47 Church Street, Barnsley, South Yorkshire S70 2AS, United Kingdom
E-mail: enquiries@pen-and-sword.co.uk
Website: www.pen-and-sword.co.uk

or

PEN AND SWORD BOOKS
1950 Lawrence Rd, Havertown, PA 19083, USA
E-mail: Uspen-and-sword@casematepublishers.com
Website: www.penandswordbooks.com

Dedicated to the memory of Cecilia Lovi, whose many letters to her cherished son brought hope and faith in a time of crisis and went on to inspire this book.

Contents

Forewords

As Holocaust survivors are becoming increasingly less able to share their memories and their experiences of the Holocaust, it is all the more important that books such as this one are written. Organisations in the field of Holocaust education and commemoration, such as the Holocaust Memorial Day Trust, where I am chair of trustees, are constantly looking for ways to ensure that Holocaust education continues once the survivors are no longer able to impart what they saw, heard, and felt during the Holocaust, no longer able to explain what it is like to be persecuted simply for an aspect of your identity – because they were Jewish.

Exploring the use of technology, on interactive websites and experiences, using artefacts and belongings including ones that survived when individuals did not, the future of Holocaust education is exciting and innovative. But, there is nothing like hearing first-hand from a survivor, in their own words, about the persecution they suffered, about the loss of their family, their home, and how the end of the Second World War and the end of the Holocaust didn't mean the end of suffering. Of course, surviving the Holocaust was an anomaly; the Nazis and their collaborators murdered more Jewish people than were able to survive. And those who were murdered are not able to share their story; in some instances, we don't even know the names of those who were murdered. Every survivor is an individual, and whilst some find sharing their story really difficult, others feel a burden to share their story as much as possible so that others can learn from and about the past.

With the diminishing numbers of survivors, it is not possible for them to reach everyone – and whilst for Holocaust Memorial Day 2022 there were more than four thousand activities taking place all over the country; the majority of these did not have a survivor present.

And that's why this book is very much needed, and could not be more timely. Marta's story, and that of her family, will now be made available to a much wider audience. Moreover, themes such as how Marta came to develop an understanding of what being Jewish meant for her and her family are crucial for our understanding of anti-Semitism, particularly as in Marta's case she rediscovered her faith as an adult, at a time when the Communist rule in Hungary not only did not teach about the Holocaust but also outlawed religion. Drawing on testimony, in the form of a cache of recently-discovered letters, this book is a rich source for all those wanting to learn not only about the Holocaust but also about the lessons that can be learned from it. Given that so much documentation from the Holocaust was lost or deliberately destroyed, having original letters enhances this book and provides a unique opportunity for the readers.

The Holocaust was a tragedy for humanity, and we all have a duty to learn both about and from the past. Despite the oft-repeated phrase 'never again', genocide has happened again and again since the Holocaust: in Cambodia, Rwanda, Bosnia and

Darfur. There are places around the world right now that are at risk of becoming genocides. But we don't need to sit by and watch as state-sponsored identity-based persecution occurs.

Individuals, organisations, community groups, all of us can take action, can work together to secure a better future, a safer future, one free from all forms of hatred. Picking up this book, reading the story is a great starting point. As Elie Wiesel, Holocaust survivor and Nobel laureate, said, listening to a witness you become a witness. Once we've read this book, we are witness to Marta's story and have a duty to share what we know, raise awareness and think about what we can do to change the future – because we all can do something. Organisations like Holocaust Memorial Day Trust have many ways to support people to both mark Holocaust Memorial Day and to engage in Holocaust and Genocide education and commemoration, but ultimately it's down to every one of us to tell the stories – and Marta's story is a great starting point.

Laura Marks OBE Chair
Holocaust Memorial Day Trust

In *Surviving the Holocaust and Stalin*, Vanessa Holburn brings us the remarkable story of survival in one family over three generations, set against some of the most tumultuous events of the twentieth century. Her sweeping narrative moves from pre-war Hungary to 1960s London and beyond in a span of over seventy years. It is a compelling story in which she highlights, as is found in other Holocaust survivors' stories, the ability of the human spirit not only to have the will to survive, but to go on surviving even after witnessing the worst cruelties and depravities man could ever inflict on fellow man. Auschwitz, Bergen-Belsen, the death marches are here given first-hand accounts in letters written on flimsy paper soon after 1945. They chart for us and for generations to come the horrors that, Lajos, Marta's father, witnessed lest ever, 'we forget'.

Soon the last of that generation of survivors will no longer be with us and it is vital that we tell and retell their stories for the next generation.

Marta Seiler inherited the family's papers on the death of her aunt and it is from the letters that this compelling book emerges. Marta's translation of these papers and letters became a truly painful experience and out of their terrible litany emerges her own plea for tolerance, eloquently argued for here in the Seilers' complex story – the endurance of two tyrannies.

From his earliest letters onwards, Lajos's personality shines through as he writes to his beloved mother from the slave labour camps to which he was deported to. And she writes back charting each deprivation as she endures it. In the details of such experience characters come vividly and poignantly alive for us.

When in 1965, at 18, Marta applied for a travel visa to go to her aunt's house in London to attend a language course, she was never to return to live in Hungary. In North London she began to observe life in a Jewish home. Gradually her awareness of her own Jewish identity grew stronger.

Arriving at a fixed identity, whatever it may be, is a crucial part of self-empowerment. My own search for a fixed identity, chartered in my memoir *Inside Out: a Life in Stages*, continues. The love match marriage in 1938 between my Ashkenazi Jewish father and my convert but very English mother still asks some questions. Better in than out? Or more outside looking in?

Happily for Marta, as she learnt more about Jewish practice and joined a synagogue, she gained her sense of self-empowerment and authenticity. However, with engagement came a sense that, like her parents, she had lost much. Theirs had been the horrifying, first-hand experience of the extremes of anti-Semitism. Hers had been the suppression of who she really was.

Strangely, and each quite distinctively, all three of them emerged as survivors.

Vanessa Rosenthal, Author
Inside Out: a Life in Stages

Introduction

When Russian tanks thundered into Ukraine in February 2022, it was an echo of the past for many in Eastern Europe. One such person was Marta Seiler, who is the force of nature behind this book. Marta's family has been caught up in the struggles that faced her birthplace of Hungary, time and time again. This book details the human cost of a nation that throughout its past has faced conflict, prejudice, extremism and totalitarianism.

Hungarian history is littered with stories of ambitious land grabs and bloody revolutions. But it has also been an accepting, diverse society, too. Like many of its neighbours, borders have shifted and populations have moved many times over. Thus it is and was a society made up of many cultures, languages and religions. Over the centuries, someone that considered themselves Hungarian might be Muslim, Jewish, Catholic or protestant. They might speak German, Latin or Hungarian, and more likely probably several languages. They could be ethnically Croat, Romanian or Turkish. Hungary's more recent history, however, shows far less tolerance and acceptance of difference.

Although her religion played a supporting rather than main role in her childhood, Marta's parents were Jewish. Because of this, her relatives met with unimaginable persecution;

persecution that would affect the rest of their lives and relationships. The Seilers were also successful business people, owning their homes, shops and other property. This too brought them into conflict and attracted punishment. Marta's stepfather was politically active, standing up for democracy and free speech at a time and in a place where this too led to violent oppression.

There have been Jews living in Hungary since the second century, with large numbers moving to Hungarian cities in the fifteenth century. While the Habsburg Empire in the late seventeenth century subjected Jews to discrimination and prohibited them from living in the major cities, by 1787 the Jewish population of Hungary had increased to around eighty-one thousand in number. By 1867 Jews were free from oppression and embedded in Hungarian commercial, financial and cultural life.[1] Marta's own relatives came to Hungary seeking suitable marriage matches within their community. They put down roots, worked hard and built up strong family and community links.

But over the centuries Hungary had got smaller and smaller. The nation has been a kingdom, part of the Ottoman Empire, part of the Habsburg dynasty and until the First World War operated under the 'dual monarchy' of the Austro-Hungarian Empire. Thus, its governments have often dreamed of clawing back territory and restoring the country to an imagined former glory. But this made it vulnerable to promises from and pacts with some of the very worst types of leaders.

From 1920 to 1946 Hungary was ruled by Regent Miklós Horthy, and relied on trade from both Italy and Germany.

Horthy was also keen to reclaim ethnic Hungarian areas in neighbouring countries and in November 1940, to help it in this aim, Hungary became the fourth member to join the Axis powers of Nazi Germany, Mussolini's Italy and the Empire of Japan. Hungary also fell into line with German policies, introducing anti-Semitic laws from 1938 that banned intermarriage between Jews and non-Jews, excluded Jews from certain professions and restricted their opportunities in economic life. By March 1944 German forces occupied Hungary. From this point on, Hungarian Jews were rounded up and sent to labour camps and Auschwitz.

Marta's family letters reveal how each stage of these discriminations affected her family. Her father was conscripted to a labour camp in ever more desperate conditions, her elderly and infirm grandmother lost her carer and personal possessions and was eventually sent to the ghetto, while her mother was transported to Auschwitz. The losses the family suffered because of government policies and actions meant that, even when they returned to their home town, their homes and businesses had been looted and their health had been permanently compromised. Anti-Semitic attitudes did not simply evaporate when the war was over.

Indeed, despite the Allies' victory, the troubles were far from over for the Seilers. By the end of the Second Word War, in return for its help in defeating Nazi Germany, and in an attempt to prevent any future German aggression, it was agreed that the Soviet Union should occupy Hungary, as well as Bulgaria, Romania, Poland and Eastern Germany. And along with its Red Army, the Stalin-led super power brought its own ideologies to its new territory, quickly reorganising the government policies to fit them. The Seilers had been business people and property owners but Stalinism did not allow for personal property and wealth. It wasn't long before nationalisation saw Marta's parents stripped of what little they had left. As her father lay dying in hospital, officials appeared at the family home and shop to claim them as their own.

The Soviets also used the available resources in Hungary to recover all that it had lost during the war. This included human labour, and many of those men in German work camps found that, rather than being liberated at the end of the fighting, they became the property instead of the Red Army and were put to work by the Soviets. About six hundred thousand Hungarians were taken to the Soviet Union as prisoners during and after the second World War[2] and since Marta's uncle remained missing after the war, a likely explanation is that he was one of them. The loss of her favourite brother was something Marta's mother never recovered from. For her there was always an empty seat at the table.

Propaganda was stepped up to encourage the adoption of Communism and acceptance of the collectivism and nationalisation enforced by the Hungarian People's Republic that ruled Hungary for the four decades from 1949. Any opposition was met with harsh penalties and brute force. Marta herself accepts that she believed what she was taught at school and became a member of the Young Communist Party. Her views were at odds with those of her stepfather, who had been raised as a Catholic and was from a farming background. Individual landowners had been forced into consolidating their fields and livestock into agricultural co-operatives. Marta's stepfather was outspoken in his beliefs and suffered the consequences.

By 1956 ordinary Hungarian citizens wanted their homes, their businesses and their land back from these uninvited 'liberators'. They wanted free elections and real democracy. The people became revolutionaries and rose up 'armed with little more than rifles and petrol bombs'.[3] Sadly, military might and tyrannical leaders overcame them, Soviet tanks turned beautiful Budapest to rubble, and thousands were slaughtered. The leader of the revolution, Imre Nagy, was captured and later hanged.

Many had hoped the West would come to help Hungary. But it did not. American leaders were caught up with domestic re-elections and the Suez crisis was raging. Just as it had done before, life carried on behind the Iron Curtain, which worked very well to hide the difficulties ordinary Hungarian people faced under Soviet rule.

For many years Marta herself did not know what had happened and what was happening to her family, simply because of who they were and what they believed. Her parents chose not to burden her with stories of the past, and not to risk her safety by encouraging her to go against Soviet policy. They made sure she had a happy childhood and that she was loved and cared for, always with a delicious meal in her belly.

And when her mother finally could, she found a way her daughter could have the safe and free life that she herself had been denied.

Now that Marta is in her seventies, she's been able to gather together her family's letters, and to translate and make sense of them. This book is a record of what this precious chain of correspondence taught Marta about her family's experience of war and 'peace'. Together we worked to tease out the stories you will read, combining them with Marta's childhood memories and her adult understanding of history and world events.

Marta's family has been persecuted time and time again for who they are, what they believe and what they have achieved. But they have got back up after each defeat and carried on, regaining both their dignity and economic safety. Despite all of this, and perhaps because of it, Marta herself believes in tolerance to all.

Marta is now keen to share what she has discovered about the suffering of the ordinary people of Hungary. When we read about historical events such as wars and leadership struggles, it's important to remember that there is always a personal sacrifice to those caught up within them. Marta considers it her responsibility as keeper of the letters to honour her family by sharing their experiences.

This is the story of the Seilers.

Seiler Family Tree

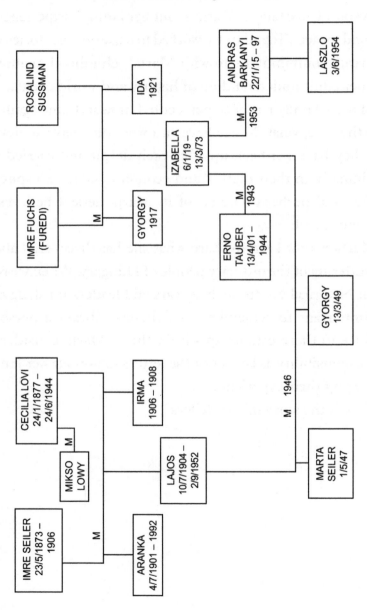

Chapter 1

Izabella, 1945, Kistelek

Izabella Tauber stepped down from the train and instinctively put her hand out to steady herself against the steel pillar of Kistelek station. She was aware her other hand was shaking. She looked at it, willing it to stop, willing herself to gather the strength to walk on. To finally walk home.

Her birthplace of Kistelek was a small town in Southern Hungary. Much of it was farming land, with a crossroads to the bigger cities at its heart. She had left Kistelek a year and a half earlier in a wooden cattle car, packed in among thirty other terrified women, bound for Szeged. Although they didn't know it at the time, from Szeged they were to be ordered onto freight trains to Auschwitz. There were many nights that she had thought she would never see Kistelek again, and some nights when she did not even want to see another dawn. But these were hazy memories of thoughts best pushed aside. Survivors don't look back. That was her way.

She had been proud of her village before, with a strong community of 400 Jews it even had its own synagogue. When she was a child it had felt safe, like home. But Hungary had become an increasingly unwelcoming place for Jews after the First World War; mass unemployment and hardship had led to anti-Semitism that seeped out and spread through the population until she and her people were just the 'stinking

Jews'. All too-willing bedfellows with Nazi Germany, by 1939 Hungarian authorities had brought in their own anti-Semitic laws. A year later all Hungarian Jewish men were conscripted into service and given a uniform. It was a policy they called *munkaszolgálat*. But instead of a gun, the men were presented with a shovel; the service they were to give their country was hard labour. It would take them far away from their loved ones, for six months at a time. They were to make the roads and the railways that would eventually be used to transport them to their death. Then Izabella watched as the pretence slipped altogether.

By 1943 all Hungarian Jews were wearing yellow stars stitched hastily to their coats. Of course, there was nothing wrong with the star itself and it didn't hurt to wear it in the same way it hurt when you were forced to your knees to beg for your life. But being forced to wear the star made it clear you were labelled as a Jew, identified as a thing to despise.

Like so many other Jewish families they knew, Izabella's grandparents had moved from Germany with their families to marry into the Hungarian Jewish community and to pursue business opportunities like the homewares shop her parents ran. They had loved their adopted country, Izabella considered herself Hungarian. But this land, ever desperate to belong to somewhere and someone since losing the power and status of its former empire, had become a slave to the Nazis and their ideals. The country's government increasingly took its lead from Berlin, regularly raiding the homes of its Jewish citizens to take with force anything they considered valuable: radios, gold, jewellery. The soldiers came every day for more and more things. How could Hungary attack its own people, Izabella had wondered? How could her fellow Hungarians join in with such relish? She felt betrayed by the people among whom she lived. The people she had called her school friends. The people she had served in the shop.

Soon Hungarian families were sent to live in homes belonging to Jewish citizens, with the original residents left huddled together in one or two of the rooms they were now legally allowed. Working for a Jew or be seen with one was forbidden, although few wanted to anyway.

Izabella herself had been married in a quiet ceremony to Erno Tauber in November 1943. It had been arranged by their parents but within six months, this hatred of Jews had made her a widow. Like all the men of his age, Erno was taken away to a labour camp, only to be beaten to death by the German guards there. Then in June 1944, aged 25, Izabella herself was rounded up with the other Jewish villagers. Any remaining men were taken away for forced labour; and the women and children sent to the outskirts of the village, to a ghetto.

There they were packed tightly into houses, thirty to forty of them in a room, fearing what would happen next. Early one morning Izabella heard shouting. She and the others were made to line up. She watched as the elderly and sick were gathered separately. From the ghetto they were taken first to Szeged, the nearest city, and from there, on to Auschwitz. Not that she knew or understood what it was when she had first arrived. How could anyone have imagined such a place?

When they were summoned, they had all grabbed their few remaining belongings, and hastily piled on any spare clothes, foolishly wondering if they would be given new homes and new lives outside the country that no longer wanted them.

How very naive we were, Izabella thought as she walked slowly through the station building and towards the door. She wondered if she would find her parents Imre and Rosalind at home. She had been separated from them in the ghetto as they waited to be sorted and had heard nothing from them since. She knew her brother Gyorgy had been taken for labour, had he returned? Had her sister Ida survived and returned to the village too? Would they be waiting for her at the shop, as though these terrible times had never happened? So many people hadn't been found yet; even she had been recorded as a missing person, located by the Red Cross, because of an enquiry made by her in-laws overseas. Families were split, everyone displaced, many had nowhere to go and no one left. It was hard to send or receive a letter. There were no papers to allow you to travel home. Many did not even want to, but she had been determined from the start to recover and return. To begin again, in spite of it all.

Later Izabella would learn that almost half of all the Jews killed at Auschwitz were Hungarian, and that they were murdered within a period of just ten weeks. She saw with her own eyes how the train tracks into the camp were deliberately extended so that the prisoners could be brought as close as possible to the chamber where they would die, with thousands gassed immediately upon arrival. Red geraniums in window boxes decorated the gas chambers to hide their true purpose. Anyone who suspected the worst and refused to walk forward was shot without hesitation. Thousands more prisoners arrived on each death train. She saw them walk in frightened but hopeful, stripped naked, expecting to shower and receive fresh clothes after their ordeal, only to be brought out lifeless on carts, now stripped of all dignity, too.

The SS soldiers that supervised the deportation of Hungarian Jews to the death camp were known as Sonderkommando Eichmann, led by an officer called Adolf Eichmann. His soldiers had arrived in Hungary on 19 March 1944 during the holiday of Purim. It seemed to Izabella that she was always running from those who wanted to torture and kill her just for the sin of being Jewish. Eichmann was obsessed with 'the Jewish problem', although the Jews hadn't been a problem when they were working hard to run the businesses the residents of Kistelek needed on their high street. Some said Eichmann wanted all Jews sent to Palestine, but that the British wouldn't allow it. Instead Eichmann devised his 'Final Solution' and organised the 'transportation to the East' of the European Jews. This is how four hundred and thirty-seven thousand Hungarian Jews came to be gassed at Auschwitz. But Izabella knew you didn't have to be a high-ranking Nazi to have a hand in this genocide, the Hungarian and German authorities, soldiers and civilians all helped. Everyone that hadn't protested, who had turned away instead of speaking out, shared this blame, this shame.

It took them three days to travel to Auschwitz. The only light and air in the cramped cattle cars came through the tiny spaces between the planks of wood and a small wired window. They were locked in with no chance of escape and little space even to move when your body cramped and ached. Some had to stand, some had no choice but to squash near the corner that passed as a toilet. When the drinking water ran out mouths grew drier and muffled cries became quieter. She wondered if she would die there. Some did, and the bodies lay among the living.

On arrival at the camp, they were separated, fates decided by seemingly random criteria. Young girls stood on their tiptoes, wondering if it would be to their advantage if they looked older and fit for work. It was hard to second guess how and why they were being judged. The captives learnt quickly as the guards passed through the crowds that the soldiers were looking only for hard workers, everyone else was expendable; as if they were donkeys at market judged only on their ability to pull a heavy cart. Young children, pregnant mothers, babies, the elderly, those that still looked well turned out with willowy figures and manicured nails were sent on their way. They stood en masse, wrapped in coats and headscarves, united by the gold star stitched to their clothes waiting for the decision that could cost them their lives, barely understanding the repercussions of which way they were sent.

Against the odds, Izabella had survived the camp. She had lived in fear, and would always live in fear, but she had lived. Together Izabella and those she had formed friendships with had faced endless days of incredible hunger and thirst, she living in relative luxury off scraps from the kitchen she had worked in, compared to others who saw only watery soup with remains of mice in, drinking their own urine in place of water, keeping clean with soap made of ashes. In these squalid conditions, your health could deteriorate rapidly and any signs of sickness meant you were sent immediately to the gas chambers. So many died every day, but her life had been spared. HER life. She owned it now.

Then, suddenly, from Auschwitz they were marched for endless days to Bergen-Belsen. If you wanted to live, and she did, you walked on and on, without complaint or rest. But more than half couldn't force themselves to walk; starved and sick with typhus and dysentery, their bodies could take no more. They died where they fell, and were left there, too. Izabella would always remember stepping over the helpless bodies as the march moved on, enduring all that she had to in order to stay alive, in spite of everything. Clenching her jaw, dipping her head against the wind.

Bergen-Belsen stank of the dying and dead. Row upon row of miserable wooden huts were encircled by barbed wire, looked over by high watch towers so that your every move was visible. And so many bodies, too many to even bury.

While Auschwitz was hell on earth, it was at least ordered, but Bergen-Belsen was in chaos. The inmates could sense the soldiers were panicking, although they never dreamed this was because other soldiers were coming to end the days of terror there. Every day more people dropped to their feet, never to stand again. Their friends were forced to carry them to the ever-growing piles of bodies across the camp. Naked bodies were everywhere, in piles, in carts, limbs hanging. The faces of the walking skeletons still yet to die would stay with Izabella forever. She knew she must never succumb, never give up, and that if she wavered in her desire to survive, she would die. If friends began to droop, you had to drag them to their feet and make the counting. If someone failed to make roll call they were taken to the crematorium.

When the British finally came, they found many of them wandering, dazed, crying with relief, some too weak even to put out their hands. Riddled with lice, crippled with disease, many of them barely clothed, those with no control over their bowels, gripping their stomachs in pain. All of them were clinging onto life any way they could.

But that was in the past, and that was where it would remain. She had stayed at Bergen with the British for six months, helping her friend Anna in her canteen, cooking for 150 people at a time. Growing stronger through her work there, physically because she could slowly learn to eat and sleep again, and mentally as she strengthened her resolve to reclaim the life that had been stolen from her. Waiting eagerly for the papers that would allow her to journey back to Kistelek.

Leaving the station, Izabella was greeted by the familiar layout of her home town and the roads that were wide enough for two cars to pass. As she came out of the station, she knew if she looked to her right she would see the timber yard, where they had collected the men, and beyond that the farm belonging to the Barkanyi family. Instead she turned left onto Rákóczi Street and towards the Saint Stephen church with its awe-inspiring Baroque tower. As a child her eyes were drawn ever upwards as she admired the unending progression to its spire. The chimes of its clock would punctuate her days. When she came to the crossroads, she knew she would then head south on Petőfi Sándo Street, where her parents' shop and her home stood. Home.

I'm here, Izabella thought as she turned, I'm finally here. I survived and I can reclaim my home and my family. We can pick up where we left off, and have our lives back again.

She took a last look down at her hands, the strong hands of a shopkeeper, hands that had always been used to hard work, the nails kept short and clean, with no time to preen or polish them.

The hands that had saved her life.

Chapter 2

Lajos, 1945, Kistelek

'It's time,' said Lajos as he stood opposite Tamás Szabó, who was in his yard sorting the little building materials he had, trying to work out how he could use them to help his neighbours repair and rebuild the village. Tamás looked apprehensive, but did what he knew was being asked, leading the smaller man to his open-backed horse cart, jumping easily up and motioning for Lajos to join him. Once Lajos was seated, Tamás glanced sideways at the former shopkeeper and tried hard not to show his shock at the grey and emaciated frame he saw there beside him.

Lajos wore a suit that had clearly belonged to a shorter man in the past, and with his ankles now visible, it was obvious he had no socks to wear and that the ill-fitting shoes he had were heavily worn, too. It was hard to believe that this was the man that had once commanded so much respect in the village, owning several shops and business, and renting out property. In fact, he was barely recognisable; he looked more like a ghost of the man he had known. Had this ghost returned for a reckoning wondered Tamás? From what Tamás had witnessed, Lajos certainly had just cause.

Lajos had owned the builder's merchants where Tamás bought his cement and paint, the tools of his trade that allowed him to earn a living as a builder, for many happy and easy years before the war. The store was a hub of activity with all the tradesmen, villagers and farmers meeting there to collect materials and discuss their projects, and life in general. Tamás had always found Lajos fair and pleasant to trade with, and being able to buy the goods locally saved Tamás the time and effort it took to drive his horse and cart over to the larger Szeged. Over time the two men had become friends. Lajos had respected Tamás's abilities, and they often fell into easy chat about how certain projects could and should be completed. Both men enjoyed the challenge a new project presented, keen to find out about any novel ways to improve working practices.

But were they still friends now, after all that had happened? Tamás wondered. Because somewhere deep in the pit of his stomach, was the nagging feeling that perhaps he had not been the friend that he should have been. And not just to Lajos, but also to all those that had been labelled undesirable.

Lajos knew he was being assessed of course. In these last few years so many had passed judgment on him, his appearance, his past and his future. He was also all too aware of his shabby appearance and slight frame. But the humiliation of being seen in this village visibly starved wearing threadbare, ill-fitting clothes paled into insignificance when compared with the horrors he had experienced. When your suffering lasts for days and months and years, you reach a point beyond which you can feel no more. You form a protective shell so that you feel nothing. And that is both a good and a bad thing.

Lajos was also used to being watched. Watched and avoided. Watched and jostled. Watched and jeered at by those that hated all the Jews. He was watched by the labour camp guards too and beaten when they decided he was not working hard enough, or maybe just because they wanted a bit of amusement to pass the long days. And there were so many of these endless days. Days stitched together with fitful sleep, his body aching with hunger and withered muscles forced to repeat the same work again and again with inadequate sustenance and no time to recover.

Of course, whether you cared about what people thought of you was greatly affected by what you thought of them.

No doubt Tamás had been in the crowd when the authorities came to Kistelek and rounded up the older or sick Jewish men, thought Lajos. When they were taken, no one had stepped forward in opposition. Suddenly the Jewish man you had stood and joked with was not a friend. In fact he was nothing, little more than a rat that could be chased away by a vermin specialist, while you feasted on the spoils. And when his scared and elderly mother was taken from their former home and into the ghetto, when he wasn't there to protect her from the rough hands of the soldiers, still no one spoke up for her, for any of them, when he couldn't. No proxy protector had stepped forward.

He could never forgive the betrayal of the silent bystanders that allowed this to happen while he toiled at the labour camp. They were as guilty as the Nyilas. Perhaps they were even worse than them, because they knew by name the people that were taken to die. They had used that name to call across the street and say a cheery good morning just months before. Lajos stared straight ahead as the horse plodded on.

In truth, Tamás knew he had let his friend down. And let down so many others in his country, too. Those first opportunities to speak up that he hadn't taken had allowed atrocities to be committed in his name. Atrocities that the people were slowly beginning to learn about fully. It started with little steps yes, but by the end of the journey, it seemed he had allowed all humanity to be abandoned. Yes, his throat was very dry as he sat next to Lajos.

Once the strict laws against Jews were introduced, Tamás was too frightened to oppose them in case his family were ostracised for being sympathisers. Suddenly Jews were forbidden to own radios and typewriters, to be involved in the running of the village or even to live in more than one room; sometimes the authorities sent German officers and their families to live in the other parts of the house. It didn't seem like too big a thing, he'd thought at the time. Plenty of Jews had plenty of money, maybe sharing it out wouldn't be all bad in these hard times, with so many still getting back on their feet after the Great War. But public opinion seemed to harden more and more and Tamás had to check how he was thinking some days, because he knew the people being penalised and he liked them, didn't he? As he listened to others discuss the changes and the new laws, it was as if the people had been given permission to pour all their hatred out onto these men, women and children. Yes, even the children were hated. How could that be right? But again, had he spoken up? The answer was no.

Tamás knew he had merely watched as the Jewish men headed off for labour camp instead of active service. And yes when the remaining Jews, mainly women and children, but also some older men who had been left behind because they were of no use to the army, were taken he had again remained silent and impotent. For his friends' sake he had hoped they were being moved to the new Jewish land that the government had spoken of, sending the fathers and husbands ahead to settle first. But perhaps he had known this was not true even then. In time he had learnt that while Lajos was working for the army his mother had to knit him socks and send him basic necessities just to keep him alive. He had heard talk recently that those that went after were less fortunate, and were not led to a new home but instead gassed in large buildings designed for this exact purpose or slowly starved in squalor. Hundreds of thousands of them people said.

And yet here was Lajos, or someone that seemed to be him, barely alive physically but able to command Tamás to drive his horse wherever he said. A ghost? A demon? A reckoning?

Lajos broke the silence. 'By the end of today my bath will be back where it should be,' he said. Tamás's throat tightened even more.

By now, Lajos had been back in Kistelek for several days, but his fury at what had happened to his home while he toiled on the railways and roads, all for the greater good of this 'glorious' Hungarian nation that he was not welcome in, had not subsided.

Lajos had been liberated from the labour camp after the Nazis were defeated but ravaged with typhus; he was immediately admitted to Budapest hospital. It was four weeks before he was well enough to be taken in by relatives in the city, who had fed him and passed on the few clothes they could spare so that he had something to wear other than the tattered and filthy rags he had arrived in. Still weak, he was determined to return to the familiar walls of his home and business. He had hoped against all odds that he might find his dear mother back there, ready to fuss over what he was eating and what he was wearing. His hope had all been in vain.

He was one of the first of the Jews to return to the village. Although in the end, there would not be many that could or did, and even less that wanted to. It was a village that he had once, foolishly now he realised, considered his home, with a community he was proud to work in and for. He arrived in Kistelek via a train from the capital, stepping down onto the platform that looked just the same despite the fact that everything had forever changed.

Lajos had known as he walked away from Kistelek station and along the side streets towards his home that day that he was again being watched. He was a thin and weak survivor walking as purposefully as his withered frame would allow through a village that was not expecting him. Curtains twitched and voices hushed as he passed by. He knew some would not welcome the sight of people such as him returning. But he did not care if they watched and he did not care if they welcomed him. He was back.

As he drew closer to his house, he had felt his knees weaken. The front door was no longer there; even the hinges were gone, prized off along with the plaster on the walls where they had been, showing how the offender had struggled to retrieve his prize. His relatives in Budapest had told him to prepare for looting but he could not imagine it happening to him, and here in the village he grew up in. Surely it was the lowest behaviour to loot the home of someone who had already lost so much.

Taking a deep breath in, he had entered and as he walked from room to room he found his home had been stripped bare. He knew, of course, that even before his mother was taken to the ghetto and on to Auschwitz that the soldiers had come time and time again and taken anything considered valuable. She had told him this much in the letters she sent every day as he worked, first just outside the village, and then increasingly further away, her letters taking on a new urgency with each of the extra kilometres. But it seemed that since then, others had come and taken whatever they fancied, and perhaps things they hadn't even wanted just for the sake of it. There was not a stick of furniture, a piece of house linen or even a single wooden spoon to be found. And perhaps worse than the government-sanctioned theft by soldiers, was the thought that these smaller things had been taken by those he had lived among, his customers, his neighbours and perhaps even his 'friends'.

The story had been the same within his shop and the 100-square-metre store at the back of his property. All his stock was gone, clearly taken by those that thought he, and his type, would never return to claim their belongings. The pattern rollers that he hired out, the materials that allowed the locals to build homes for their loved ones, the hard-to-find goods his mother had stocked at the beginning of the war so their customers would not go without. Items not asked or paid for, but simply stolen without a sense of remorse or the thought they would be caught and punished for such an act. An act clearly no one considered a crime because the victim was a Jew.

His home, his shop; emptied. And perhaps, in some ways, his heart, too.

Now at night Lajos slept on a bare floor without a sheet. It was far from comfortable but still one hundred times better than life in the labour camp, where every day he wondered if it was his last. Typhus had left his body weak, but even when he could not sleep through anger and fear and pain, he could at least rest, knowing that the next day would not be filled with the sound of his shovel endlessly hitting the ground, grit in his eyes, lice in his hair. If he wanted to lie still when the sun first rose, he would be able to do so. There was no one here to wake him with the kick of a steel-tipped boot to the head and a harsh command.

But if he had been angry as he walked through the bare kitchen, living room and bedrooms of his home on that first day back, it was nothing compared to the rage he had felt when he came to the bathroom. His most prized room of all of those in his home and especially important to his mother. Across the back of the room was nothing but space. There was no water tank above the fire and the pipework had been left hanging loose, dangling hopelessly as if it too understood what is was to be the persecuted. Someone had stolen the bath.

The bath was no ordinary thing. It was not like a saucepan, a stove or even a kitchen sink. Any person might have those. The bath was extraordinary, a real one-of-a-kind, and here in Kistelek, plumbed into his house the bath had meant everything to him and his mother, Cecilia. By taking it, the thief had taken more than a desirable possession and it was more than Lajos could bear.

Lajos had procured the full-length glistening white enamel tub in the city, bringing it back carefully by cart alone. He and Tamás had worked together to figure out how the fire would heat the tank and how a pipe would take away the resulting smoke so the room remained comfortable and safe. Then they connected the pipes so that when the taps were opened hot water ran freely into the bath below. It was a magnificent piece of engineering. It was the future. And Lajos had brought it to the village first.

The bath with its ready supply of running hot water was the height of luxury and had been a tangible symbol of his family's hard work and wealth. It was quite the talk of the village and complimented the English toilet they also owned, another item that was unusual at that time. His mother was so proud of the bath, cleaning it carefully after each use, so that it was always shiny when visitors came to gaze at it. Which they did, no one was too shy to ask to see this wonderful thing.

It was not hard to discover who had the bath now, because it was still a rarity to possess such a symbol of refinement. Perhaps more so since the war had taken the men away and stifled business. He had gone straight to ask Tamás, because apart from himself, Tamás was the only other person in the village who knew how to remove and install such an advanced item. And this meant that Tamás was in some way implicated in its disappearance, too. Tamás confessed immediately that yes, he had helped with both the removal and re-installation, and that the bath was now in the house of the local dentist, András Kovács. And as he spoke, Tamás's cheeks had burned with shame.

Lajos had reported each and every one of his stolen items to the police and asked around the neighbourhood for his typewriter. He was not embarrassed; although those he spoke to about his missing possessions often struggled to hold his gaze. Although he didn't expect to receive many of his things back, he wanted the thefts acknowledged and officially recorded. Because taking his items was a crime, whoever and whatever he was.

But with the bath, his bath, it was different.

Although he had known the whereabouts of the bath for several days, Lajos had waited until everything was in place before he visited the dentist. He wanted to ensure the removal would go smoothly and there would be no reason for the bath not to be back in its rightful home by sunset. He set off to Tamás's house to collect him knowing the removal and installation was still a two-man job. Although, he thought, the true definition of 'man' surely meant something more than just the physical abilities of someone?

From there they rode to the Kovács' house, the cart would be necessary to transport the bath.

The dentist had not tried to argue when confronted, stepping aside sheepishly as he opened his door. Perhaps he knew Lajos was coming anyway, maybe Tamás had warned him. Were non-Jews now closer to each other, united in their actions, and more likely, guiltily united by their inaction? Would Jews continue to be the 'outsiders'?

Because Lajos had ensured he had both the know-how and the manpower to remove the bath, and the means to transport it, by the day's end, his bath was reinstalled in his house.

While the rest of the rooms still lay barren, the bathroom was once again a testimony to what Lajos had, could and would achieve. He smiled for the first time in a long while.

This day would not be last time his forethought and ingenuity helped him to survive and recover. He was not beaten, he would rebuild.

Chapter 3

Marta, 1957, Kistelek

Marta is awake and since it is winter when she breathes out she can make her own tiny cloud of fog. She's not sure why she's awake but keeps all of her body tucked carefully underneath her heavy, goose down duvet, trying not to move. She knows that the thick inside layer will have shifted to the bottom end of her cover while she slept, just as it always does. When she packs it away in the morning she will shake it firmly to break up the clumps of down so it is ready for the next night. She is now 10 years old and since her stepfather was taken there's lots she has to do to help her mother keep the house and the boys in order.

Her room is inky black and she realises there is tapping at her window breaking through the silence. She is surprised but not scared that this has woken her. How odd that someone should call this late at night, or perhaps it is early morning, she thinks. The window opens only to the yard that runs between their neighbours, the Kiss family, and her family house. She does not know how anyone has passed through the high metal gates that border their home to allow them just a little privacy from the eyes of the authorities. When the gates are closed her parents know they can meet whomever they like and listen ever so quietly to any radio station they choose.

Pretty lace curtains frame the window, hanging softly from the rail where metal circles with pegs are clipped to the flowered gauze. The curtains are white cotton, just like all the bed linen in the house. Marta knows her father worked hard so he could replace all their belongings with only the very best because they had been stolen and looted during the war when everyone thought they'd seen the last of the Jews. She also understands that because of the new rules, her mother is not allowed to work, so instead she washes, starches and irons the bed linen very regularly. Marta knows her mother is cross that she can't get a job, but never discusses it with her; after all, speaking up is why her stepfather isn't home anymore. Mother's hard work, however, means when Marta goes to bed, slipping between the carefully laundered sheets feels to her like sinking into a safe, warm embrace.

The curtains are never drawn, and her mother says that they are more for looking at than using, things of beauty from 'before', so when she undresses at night she does so without the light on to make sure no one can see her. Although there is a large tiled stove here in the middle room where she sleeps, it is never used and the room is cold. It's also the dining room that the family uses for celebrations and formal gatherings, although Marta realises that they don't have many of those at the moment. She also knows they can't share food they don't have and there seems very little to celebrate, too.

At night her mother sleeps on the sofa bed in the living room, where most of the furniture and possessions are kept. It's the warmest room with its black metal coal heater, and so it's also where Marta must study. When the weather gets better in a few months, the family will swap their heavy duvets over to the lighter quilts, with their shiny satin covers. Marta's brothers share the bedroom beyond hers; Gyuri (real name Gyorgy) in the bed, and her half-brother Laci (Laszlo to the grown-ups) in a cot.

Gyorgy was named after her mother's older brother, who Marta knows her mother worries about no end. Her uncle is one of the many that are 'missing' and the family can't find him anywhere despite years of looking. Her mother speaks about him to Marta all the time. He was older than her, and protective, always calling her his 'Baba', a pet name that stuck even as she grew up, so much so, few people knew Izabella's real name. Marta finds it hard to imagine her mother as the one being taken care of; because it's her mother that makes sure they are all fed and cared for. Before she married András, Marta knew that her mother had nursed her father with the same compassion she showed her children, too. She wasn't a warm woman, or a mother that showed her feelings easily but somehow you knew that if Izabella loved you she would make sacrifices to see you fed and clothed.

The last thing Marta's mother knows about her brother Gyorgy is that, like all the healthy Jewish men, he was collected and taken away to work for the army. Much later, after the Germans had been defeated, someone from his work section made it back to the village. But many of those who were in the labour camps never returned, and people say they were not liberated by the Russians at all, and had to keep working just as hard but simply for a different master.

Marta doesn't want to leave her nice warm spot to find out who is calling, although she's always pleased when people get to see her pyjamas. She and her siblings receive a new pair every single year when they celebrate Télapó, which the people must now have in place of Christmas because the government says so. At the very last minute her mother will place gifts under the family Christmas tree in the room where she sleeps and in the morning the children rush to see which pile is whose. The tree has sweets wrapped in paper tied to its branches, and the children sneak out of bed at night to unwrap and eat these little treats, carefully wrapping up the empty paper and rehanging it so their mother doesn't notice. The children wonder why when Télapó is over, their mother never seems to notice that all the sweets are now gone. Perhaps she believes in Télapó magic, they reason.

As well as the new set of pyjamas, the children sometimes also get a juicy orange, which Marta likes to peel in one go, so she can have a long coil of pimply skin. One year she got a banana instead of the orange but she didn't like it and neither did her brothers. It was green and hard and they found it bitter. Their mother ate all three in the end. Sometimes the children get a reading book too. They use the library regularly but actually owning a book is special. Marta's brother's favourite story is *The Last of the Mohicans* but she prefers *Huckleberry Finn*.

Marta wonders if the person at the window is wearing pyjamas or if they have got up and got dressed already today. Perhaps they haven't even been to bed yet, she thinks? Even at her young age she knows they live in a time of secrets, and she's not sure if you are allowed out on the streets at night-time. She also knows that not everyone follows the rules all the time and is aware that people in her neighbourhood travel in cars to Czechoslovakia to sell the food they have produced on the black market, staying overnight and returning secretly with the textiles they manufacture over there. Of course, Marta realises this is something else that you mustn't talk about. And since she wants to make sure she has new pyjamas next Télapó too, she'll happily keep the secret.

Marta wriggles her legs free, placing them on the rug that stretches from under the dining table, and edges toward her bed. Placed atop the chevron patterns of the parquet floor, the rug deadens any sound her bare feet might make as she moves towards the window. There are two layers of glass, with a six-inch gap between the panes. As she opens the first window she can just make out the shape of a head, but she can't see any more. She finds the air is even colder as she reaches forward. Then her mother enters the room and, gently moving her aside, swiftly opens the second window and stretches out both her hands, clearly expecting both the visitor and to receive something from them. When she brings her hands back in, Marta can see she holds a large roughly-woven basket. Marta's mother shuts the window quickly without speaking to the shady figure, and Marta never gets to see who it is that has delivered the basket.

'Go back to sleep!' her mother whispers to Marta as she turns, but in a tone that tells Marta she really means it. She does as she is told without saying a word; she knows better than to ask questions when her mother looks like this. In fact, she knows better than to ask too many questions anyway, as she's already found that grown-ups don't like her asking questions.

Back in bed, Marta wonders what kind of delivery comes at night. Although she could see the basket was full, she couldn't make out exactly what with because of the dark. She recognises that the willow basket had handles just like the ones the farmers' wives carry in the village, and knows that her family are in some way connected to the village farming families. She's also aware that her stepfather has relatives that subtly check in on them now he is gone. But she knows too that the police keep a watchful eye on the farmers, as lots of things aren't allowed, like keeping your own animals or helping the bourgeoisie, which is what Marta and her family are. The farmers are now organised into communes, because property has been nationalised. Each commune has a specific task to complete and is run by someone that the authorities trust. The farmers are not happy that they can no longer work for themselves, and instead are allocated a proportion of what the commune produces overall. But Marta's teachers have told her that communism is a great system, and so she figures it must be true, after all, why would teachers lie? And if people really weren't satisfied they would speak up, right?

Marta remembers the time before now, when the family used to be rich and owned the house they lived in and the shop to its front. She knows that before the war, and before the Russians came, that her real father's family had several shops and owned lots of buildings, too. She's also been told that all their belongings were taken from the family by the Germans because they were Jewish but after the war more changes and punishments came because of what they owned, too. Good communists, she has learnt, don't own property and must share everything, working for the common good. Now everything is state owned, which school tells us is for the good of everyone, whatever their race, whatever their job. Although somehow being bourgeoisie does mean you get less. And everything seems harder because everyone has less in Hungary now. It was all very confusing.

Marta thinks back to last year when everyone in the village had matching red skirts because the clothes factory only had red fabric. This year the factory only has blue material. How funny to see everyone dress the same.

Marta remembers the day she came home from school to find that the police had bricked up the doorway between the house and the business. Her mother told her the men had shown her a piece of paper, and told her that if the family wanted to stay they would have to pay rent to the government because they owned it now. That night she heard adults cursing the communists again and again and her mother shushing them in case Marta caught what they were saying and told someone about the views they expressed.

Marta misses sitting on the steps of the shop though, watching the customers come and go, each choosing different items and enjoying chatting to her parents and the other villagers freely. Now bread, sugar, flour and meat are rationed and luxuries are frowned upon, when people shop there are no smiles and small talk. Marta knows that Hungarians are resourceful, however; her neighbours grow parsley, which they share with them, and an old man finds mushrooms in the forest for the family, bringing them in a huge basket. And her mother knows how to tweak the dishes she prepares to make a tasty meal.

When Marta wakes again it is light enough for her to see the pale yellow walls of her room. She can hear her mother in the room next door, although it is quieter now her stepfather isn't here. He always rose at 5am, and he and her mother would sit at the square table in that room, with its vinyl cover, chatting together over hot tea and cigarettes.

This morning though Marta can smell food cooking, which is unusual. Normally the family eats bread spread with fat, and maybe a spoonful of sugar sprinkled on the top if they have it. They drink only tea or water. If Marta's mother baked on the coal stove the day before, they might have leftover cake in the morning, too, and when they are ill they are allowed an egg to help them get better. But from what she can smell now, today must be special, as special as a birthday she thinks. She's eager to get to the kitchen and see what is going on, but must get washed and dressed and pack away her bed first. Then she must get her younger brother up and dressed for nursery, which he has recently started.

At last the children are ready and can go and find their mother at the other side of the house. As ever, the pine rectangle table where they eat breakfast is pushed up against the wall. It's a working table; Marta's mother prepares their food on it and scrubs it clean daily, moving in wide circles across the pine. But this morning Marta can scarcely believe her eyes. The table is laden with smoked sausage, bread, eggs and milk. Her stomach lurches with hunger and she feels her mouth soften as any trace of overnight dryness evaporates. The mismatched white plates and the heavy cutlery await the siblings, inviting them to the feast before them. Their mother stands to one side smiling broadly. Marta exchanges glances with her brothers and they don't wait for a formal invite but sit down swiftly, more than ready to eat this unexpected banquet.

When they have finished eating, their tummies feel fuller than they have ever been. Everyone is quiet and content. As Marta looks at my mother she seems softer than normal somehow, her brow less furrowed. She thinks of the night-time guest and understands that these two events are linked.

But who was the visitor Marta wonders? And why did they bring the food? How did they have such items when everything is rationed and accounted for? Was this the first time a basket of such things has been delivered? Will it come again? But as much as she is curious, she instinctively knows that what she saw last night must never be spoken of. She knows her many questions about the night-time visitor, the morning's feast and how the two are connected, must never be asked.

Marta also knows that there are many things her mother doesn't want to talk to her about, many things that she hides, even from her eldest child. It seems to Marta that their lives are shaped by what they don't and what they can't say; the things that happened in the past that they mustn't mention, and the secret things that happen now.

Marta wonders if her mother will ever speak freely to her.

Chapter 4

Marta, 1965, Kistelek

'If I never see you again, I will be happy, because I know you will have a better life,' Izabella whispered to her daughter.

They were standing together at the bus stop on Petofi Sandor Street, Marta clutching the handles on her suitcase rather too tightly and very much wishing the bus would come right on schedule as it usually did. Marta could feel the warmth of the sun on her back but shivered at the tone in her mother's voice. The national bus service was both reliable and well used, although like all of Hungary at the time, friendliness wasn't a given. Faces were always sour, shortages were the norm and Marta's stepfather always said even the simple things such as obtaining a screw for a household job required five journeys. Getting on that bus would still be more enjoyable than this conversation though, thought Marta.

It felt strange to be here so early in the morning and even to be alone with her mother. As the eldest child, she was used to taking responsibility for her siblings and working alongside her mother in their busy household. But it was early September and school had restarted for both her brothers, with Gyorgy already having left Kistelek for his studies elsewhere a few days before. Unusually this meant the two of them had unhurried time together. And now this!

Marta wasn't used to her mother being open about her feelings and this unfamiliar ground was definitely outside of her comfort zone. Instead 18-year-old Marta was focused on enjoying her trip to England and avoiding conversations like this one. She looked again down the road, as if there were something in the distance, simply to avoid her mother's gaze. She was only going overseas to fill in some time before deciding what to do next, she thought to herself. Her mother's sentiment seemed both wholly unnecessary and uncomfortably out of character.

Marta knew the journey ahead would be a long one but it had been meticulously planned, with relatives and friends due to meet her along the way, helping her to navigate the cross-city transfers and providing water and sustenance, since there would be no opportunity to buy more supplies along the route. The buffet cart on the train to England was reserved for the use of first-class passengers only (she was second class, no change there) and Hungarian currency wasn't accepted outside the country anyway.

Her first stop would be at around midday in Budapest, where she would need to make it to the railway station and board the train to Vienna. It would be evening when she reached the Austrian capital and there she must take the connection to London, which meant alighting at Calais so that the passengers could take the ferry to the English coast and continue on to Charing Cross by train. She was expected by the evening of the 5th. That would be two whole days of travelling alone through many countries when previously

Marta had barely ever left her village. Marta found it both exciting and terrifying. She couldn't imagine what these places would be like, as the Hungarian government was reluctant to engage with the parts of Europe that supported capitalism and information about the West was therefore limited.

Staying with her aunt in London hadn't been part of Marta's plans for the future. She'd wanted to study law at university after school, but despite her excellent A-level grades in History, Russian and Maths, no place had been forthcoming. Like many of her friends who also found further education inaccessible, she hoped to apply again the following year. Under the communist system university teaching was free of course, but you had to attend your closest university, and were expected to live at home, travelling in for lessons each day. Because of this Marta knew she'd need a part-time job to support herself while she studied, and could see that she and her friends were yet another generation that learnt how to work hard and get by.

She also knew that even after graduation your career wouldn't necessarily bring wealth even in those professions that were highly regarded. It was typical at that time when visiting a doctor or receiving nursing care in a hospital to come ready with envelopes stuffed with cash. Marta had always been told that to encourage attention from a consultant or to get your dressings changed promptly, you'd need a little something extra to offer as an incentive. She could only guess that the staff in hospitals were as financially stretched as everyone else, living the same existence.

Marta knew from listening to her mother that her aunt had always wanted to move her parents to England, but when that became impossible because of restrictions set by the Hungarian government she had instead offered to pay for Marta's younger brother to come to her rooms in St John's Wood. When the offer fell to Marta simply because she was at a loose end that year, Gyorgy wasn't happy, feeling his sister had snaffled his opportunity before he had a chance to finish school and take Aranka up on it.

Aunt Aranka was the older sister of Marta's father and had married in Vienna in 1939. She had made it to England by boarding the last train out of her home city before Hitler closed the border. At the time, she was married to a rich timber merchant called Isaac Weiss and had never worked a day in her life. Although to the family left behind, Aranka's life overseas seemed charmed, instead of the large apartment and wealthy lifestyle she had enjoyed before the war, Aranka rented rooms in a shared house and even shared a bathroom with the other tenants. Marta's aunt and uncle had sacrificed everything they owned to flee the Germans as they advanced across Europe and to stay alive, but later the family would see that her uncle suffered debilitating depression for the rest of his life because of the upheaval. Aranka, however, had managed to get on with earning a living and starting a new life, even if she had been used to so much more.

Once in England, Aunt Aranka had found work at a milliners in Luton, renting a room to live in. They became firm friends with a Czech couple they met, called Friedle and Eric Flux. The bookkeeper husband was Jewish and that had helped them forge a lifelong connection. After the war, Friedle and Aranka were confident enough in the trade to open their own business and moved to London to set up in South Molton Street. Sat on one of the smartest streets in London, their shop was near the only place that sold proper coffee in the city, which Marta found you could smell all the way to Bond Street. Her aunt's business, Ari Hats, did well, and she loved to see the labels with her brand sewn into the inside of the brim. Ari Hats even supplied pieces to the milliner to the Queen, Frederick Fox, which in turn led to the aristocracy taking an interest in having a hat from Aunt Aranka too. What an accolade ... and a good selling point! Friedle became one of Marta's aunt's best friends and they developed their own set of customers to attend to; Friedle the younger stylish crowd, Marta's aunt the older ladies. It was an exciting time to be in London, and for Marta it was the key to whole new lifestyle, where commerce not communism brought happiness and opportunity.

It hadn't been a simple process for Marta to leave Hungary, the government tried to make it as difficult as it could. However, Aranka had agreed to pay for an English course so that her niece could improve her spoken language skills and then take the Cambridge Language Exam at the end of her studies. This in turn would allow Marta to apply for a visa from the British authorities, and because the language course was already booked Marta was given a student visa lasting nine months.

But first Marta had to obtain a passport from the Hungarian government, as each trip overseas required a new one. And the authorities weren't always forthcoming. The regime wasn't keen on its citizens leaving and tasting life overseas, anxious that its comrades wouldn't return. To obtain a passport, you were required to provide information about your entire family and the government even wanted proof of the invitation to stay that Marta's aunt had extended. There was also the worry that her family history might adversely affect any interactions with the authorities. Luckily Marta's somewhat naive involvement in the Young Communist movement helped her obtain a reference that supported her claim that this was not just an escape plan and that she would return when her trip was over.

For her part, Marta didn't think through anything further than her planned 'language' trip; she was young and excited and heading to the West! She simply intended to pass some time enjoying England before she returned for a university place, hoping this time to get on a course of her choice.

Little did Marta know that she would shortly be arriving in one of the trendiest areas of London in the middle of a cultural revolution. Her aunt lived in Abbey Road and the Beatles' recording studio was just opposite her home. With limited radio reception in Kistelek, Marta was largely uninformed about the world outside her tiny village with its one grocery shop and close-knit community. Perhaps unbelievably, the phrase Beatlemania meant nothing to her. To say that she would find moving from Kádár-era Hungary to the Swinging Sixties a culture shock is an understatement. There was some consistency in her life, however; she slept on a sofa bed in her aunt's living room and each morning she packed away her bed, just as she had done throughout her childhood.

But it was time to leave her childhood behind. Marta's life was about to begin afresh.

Chapter 5

Lajos and Izabella, 1946, Kistelek

Lajos sat at his typewriter, finally able to relay good news to his sister. Here at the makeshift desk in his broken home, he had tried so often to put into words so many of the things he was unable to say out loud.

Through his past correspondence he had told Aranka how he had seen their mother's health decline before the war and how he was taken away to the labour camp for that final time. He described how Cecilia's desperate letters to him showed she had faced constant harassment once he was away, with soldiers coming several times a day to take their belongings. Eventually, she was moved to the ghetto with the other remaining Jews. He spoke too of his despair that he had not been there to protect her from these harsh experiences.

At times he could not believe his luck that he still had his sister and her husband safely in England to write to. It was a welcome outlet despite the first news he had to tell her had been the sure death of their dear mother, most likely in the wagon on her journey to Auschwitz. So many from their village had not returned either. He listed the families so that she could know who was and wasn't here anymore. It was a sobering roll call of fractured families and interrupted lives.

He wrote, too, of his physical battles with typhus, pneumonia and a perforated stomach, and of the emotional battles he faced as he struggled to come to terms with all that he had lost. All that was taken.

Sometimes he felt guilty that he burdened his remaining family with his accounts but the relief that came from sharing and the need to tell the truth now that he could outweighed that initial emotion.

But now, less than six months after writing to Aranka that nobody could help him gain back what he was missing, everything had changed.

Izabella Tauber, or Izabella Furedi as he had known her, had returned to the village and she had shown him the path to the future. A future full of hope.

He felt sure Aranka would remember Izabella from their school days together, how could anyone not recall a woman such as her? Against all odds, Izabella had survived both Auschwitz and Bergen-Belsen and, having worked in a restaurant in Germany for six months after liberation, when she arrived in Kistelek she looked strong and healthy. Imagine a Jew that did not return a shadow of their former self but with her head held high hopeful of finding her family and her home. Lajos had been instantly in awe of her capabilities. In a typically brave mood, Izabella had her death camp tattoo removed and put the painful past behind her. He had nothing but admiration for her strength and force of personality. Discrimination, deprivation and desperation had not beaten her.

Compared to this masterpiece, Lajos considered himself wretched. He knew well enough that his mother had spoiled him, and as a result he couldn't cook or keep what there was left of his house. He also realised that if he was to recover and rebuild his business he must gain both weight and strength. He was not much of a man at 47 kilos. And certainly not the man he had been or could be. While he initially had his cousin's help and loyal neighbours in the Kiss family, now he was alone he needed to do more than just survive. He needed to live. He needed to flourish. And in doing so move from victim to victor. It was the way to prove the Nazis and their collaborators had failed.

And so Izabella had come to work for him. Initially she began to cook his meals, as up until now, he had eaten only cold food unless he ate a warm dinner at a local café. When Izabella came to his kitchen she brought with her a basic camping stove. Somehow on this simple burner she produced the most amazing succour. And carefully and slowly, which was essential so that he did not require further surgery, his belly began to grow. He could never tell if the warmth he felt spreading there while he and Izabella ate together was because of the temperature of the food, or something more.

Izabella had also proved that she could turn her hand to most things. His house began to look like a home once more, and she managed the paint business by herself so that he could concentrate on buying more building materials to reignite that side of his trade. She was resilient, intelligent and beautiful. She had just two dresses and yet was always well presented. Like him, she had lost so much during the war – a husband, a brother, years of her youth – and yet her focus remained firmly fixed on the future.

Izabella was simply wonderful, and so he had proposed. And she had accepted.

The Rabbi married them in March. There had been no photos, no banquet, and the bare minimum of witnesses as Jewish law dictated. But that night, instead of heading off to her mother's home at the end of a full day in his home and his shop, Izabella stayed behind here as his wife. Now it was their home, their shop and their future.

How he wished he had a photo of his new wife at his side to send to his sister.

* * *

Izabella worked quietly in the kitchen, delicately stirring the onions until the pale skin became translucent, then complementing the mellow taste with a teaspoon of caraway seeds waiting for the familiar anise aroma to fill the air. Next she would add the red paprika, then water, sliced potatoes and seasoning, bringing all this to the boil. She was confident it would make a delicious dish. She knew it was a recipe that was best cooked gently and slowly to better develop the deep flavours. The couple ate their main meal in the middle of the day, and Izabella had already collected the 200g ration of bread to accompany the paprika potatoes.

She smiled as she thought of her new husband tapping away at his typewriter, bought as soon as he could find one because his handwriting was so hard to read. Then she stopped and corrected herself. Lajos was not her 'new' husband; he was simply her husband. She had made up her mind that there was to be no more mention of her previous marriage to Erno Tauber. She would pack that part of her life away, along with the hellish memories of concentration camp that disturbed her sleep still, and move on.

Erno had been called up earlier than many, and as an older man, a full eighteen years older than her in fact, he had not survived the beatings at his work camp. Their arranged marriage had lasted just seven months before he was conscripted and then killed, and Izabella had not had chance to fully accept the match she had been reluctantly shoehorned into, let alone settle into being his wife in such turbulent times. Later she would dig out the photo of them together on their wedding day and carefully tear away Erno, leaving just the image of her 24-year-old self in her beautiful long white dress and veil. Much later still her daughter would find the photo and uncover many of her mother's secrets and silences.

Izabella had accepted her parents' matchmaking because there was a dearth of eligible Jewish men locally and she had married Erno as they suggested. But she had been very much in love with a local farming boy. Unlike Erno, this boyfriend was her age and lived in the village. Unlike Izabella, however, he was a Catholic and being with him was out of the question. Instead she had put aside any girlish notions of romantic love and became a Jewish wife as was expected of her. How far away that time felt.

And now here she was again, married to another older man because of a decision taken, in all honesty, for mainly practical reasons, too. But this time Izabella was hopeful for their future together. She viewed marriage so differently now. She was no longer a girl; she was a woman, and a strong one, too.

Of course, Izabella had known of Lajos Seiler before the war and its aftermath and the shared recovery that drew them together. The Jewish community in her village was tight knit back then too and the Seiler family was very prominent within it. Everyone knew that the Seilers had the only indoor toilet and hot water bath in Kistelek. The Seilers owned several businesses and properties and Lajos would have been a great prize for any bride. Indeed, Izabella's mother, perhaps rather ambitiously, had tried to broker a marriage between her daughter and Lajos through their mutual connections with no success. At that time however, it seems that Lajos's beloved mother had wanted something more for her precious son. In fact, Izabella suspected her mother-in-law had been somewhat of a snob where a potential match was involved. As it was, Lajos and his mother had never found a suitable woman for him and he had remained unmarried. Perhaps Lajos had never wanted or needed to get married while he had his mother's full attention and care, Izabella mused. After all, much as she cared for Lajos, his ability to look after himself was sadly lacking.

But now his mother was gone and he had met Izabella. And he worshipped the ground she walked on. Izabella felt her cheeks flush. How funny the way life's twists and turns can work out, she thought.

For her part Izabella was realistic though. She knew that Lajos was not the love of her life, those days had passed, but she was still happy to be his wife. In the last two years, she had survived victimisation, starvation, torture and poverty. She had proved she was resilient and strong. She had discovered she had an ability to adapt to what was asked of her, becoming a cook at Auschwitz, a role that had probably saved her life. And she found she survived best as a team, happy to share the little she had, like the vegetable peelings scavenged from those wretched camp kitchen bins. These traits had carried her through the despair and brutality of the war.

Now these characteristics had won her the devotion of dear Lajos. Here in the tatters of her former life, she had cooked and cared for a broken man. In return she discovered an unexpected romance with a partner that loved her with the sort of passion she had long since forgotten existed. Looking at herself through his eyes she saw a woman that was capable of recovery, reinvention and release. A woman that was capable of anything, whatever life threw at her. She knew now she had an inner strength, and that it could not be beaten from her.

Now they spent their days together planning the future. Building up a business and building up a home. She worked in the shop selling painting supplies while Lajos took care of the tradesmen and their materials. She cooked for Lajos, and nursed him back to health. When they had spare time, they would visit the furniture markets with the gold Lajos had so carefully concealed during the war, using only a little at a time. Hyperinflation meant that money was next to useless. They bought practical furniture but also knickknacks that would show their home was one made with love and attention. A pale watercolour of a woman sat on the steps of her farmhouse, idly feeding chickens, now hung in the hall, a heart-shaped key holder was suspended on string near the front door and an ornament of a young boy in a tall blue top hat tempting a rabbit towards him, a gun hidden behind his back, was placed proudly in the main room. Simple little trinkets yes, but they gave them huge pleasure.

Yes she was lucky to have survived the war, she knew that; after all, so many had not. But surviving was not enough for Izabella or Lajos. When she'd returned, things had not been easy and while the war was over, the fight was not. She was relieved to find her family waiting in Kistelek, of course; it made the sacrifice of turning down an invitation to work and live in England in favour of coming home to see if they were there easier to bear. But her father was gravely ill and her mother not much better. Her sister had also survived the war and quickly got married and away from her decimated family, moving on in her life. But her beloved brother was missing, and there was still no news despite all their enquiries. She missed her dear Gyorgy so much and knew she would not rest until she found him, even if it took the rest of her days.

When she returned, the village that had been her home was far from hospitable. The inhabitants were clearly afraid of those Jews that returned. And well they might be, Izabella thought with her lips pursed, for it was these former neighbours, colleagues and even friends that had allowed the Kistelek Jews to be rounded up and driven out, in many cases to their death, and in all cases to misery and malnourishment. It was also these villagers that had happily taken, well in truth stolen, the belongings and even the very houses she and her people had been dragged from, as they were left unguarded behind.

With her family home and shop empty, her parents too ill to care for themselves properly, and no Gyorgy to help,

Izabella woke everyday wondering if they would starve even though they were no longer interned. After her father died, Izabella grew more desperate until she found work with Lajos. That she had the power to heal this man through her cooking and care made Izabella feel as if she had been blessed with a certain gift. And to see the love grow in Lajos's eyes as he grew stronger was also a blessing. It was as if she was the sunshine that allowed Lajos to bloom. The woman that had once not been good enough, was the very thing he needed to live.

Before too long, Lajos had asked for her hand. Lajos was aware that she had been married before, and also that the paperwork was not in order for her to officially marry again. But this did not deter or bother him. Instead the couple opted for a religious ceremony to mark their union, planning to sort out the legalities later whenever it became possible. Izabella no longer considered herself religious, after all God hadn't exactly shown himself to his people had he? What kind of fool would worship a being that allowed hate to overpower every morsel of human goodness? But a service in the synagogue was what was on offer, so she took it.

On their wedding day she had worn one of her only two dresses; a new one was out of the question even if she had the money to buy one, as no one in Hungary had new clothes anymore. But when she caught Lajos smiling at her as the Rabbi spoke, Izabella knew that to Lajos she looked as beautiful as any bride dressed in silk and lace could. She knew too that his letter to Aranka would be full of joy and happiness, because that was what he would say about how he felt about his marriage to her to anyone that would listen. The feeling of being so treasured after being an outcast for so long was a salve to smooth over the wounds of the past.

The secret to their happiness, Izabella thought to herself as she lifted her head to look at her husband as he sat typing, was that she and Lajos shared the same outlook. They saw no reason to look back at all that had happened, they instead only wanted to focus on moving forward. They would battle together to make the future that life had tried to rob them of. It was as if their marriage vows were a commitment to the hope they were both so determined to have. She had nothing but hope for their marriage and their life together. Maybe even children she thought.

But Izabella's life never went as it should, and she would once again need to prove herself to be strong and resourceful.

Chapter 6

Izabella, 1953, Balastya

She had married out of duty, she had married out of hope and now Izabella was to marry out of love. Somehow, some way, her childhood sweetheart had been restored to her. Yes, it seemed that life's cruelty might be finally over and she could feel hope rising in her heart once again. As she tucked a loose strand of hair into her chignon and readied herself to greet the assembled guests, she wondered if this was her reward for all that she'd achieved despite what she had had to endure.

Smiling at her reflection one last time in the mirror that hung crookedly in the dusty kitchen alongside a multitude of practical pots and pans, Izabella decided from now on that 24 October 1953 would be the turning point of her life. Today on the farm in Balastya, where she'd arrived on the dirt track in a simple horse and cart, she would marry András. There would be plenty to eat, with chickens rounded up and killed for the occasion, and music would play. Her children would run among the fields with the other farmers' families, the women dressed in aprons and headscarves, and they would all be made to feel welcome. Truly welcome.

Glancing down at herself, she saw a tiny thread. Her dress was one of the second-hand ones dear Aranka had sent her, and it had been altered so that it fitted perfectly. While this wedding did not have the pomp and ceremony of her first, it was not as makeshift as her second. In fact, this time her marriage was everything she would have chosen herself: a groom she already loved and admired, and happy, smiling faces and full tummies all around. After the wedding András would leave behind this farmhouse with its low ceilings and come and live with her, Gyorgy and Marta in Kistelek, and this would help with the rent she had struggled to meet. Life would be complete. Life would be straightforward. Life would begin again. Again.

Izabella had met András as a carefree girl, which seemed a lifetime ago. Four years older than her, he wasn't tall, but he was muscular from his manual labour on the farm. From a large family, that started the days with a shot of home-made peach or apricot *pálinka*, he was typically Hungarian, pale and slim. Yes, his world was small and simple but she saw he had a big heart and she was instantly smitten. Since he had left school at 14 to work the land, András was often sent to the village for supplies and seemed to make a point of visiting her parents' shop when he knew she would be working there. They stole furtive glances at each other across the shelves. She was a middle-class Jew, he a Catholic peasant, the Romeo to her Juliet.

Of course, with their different backgrounds and social standing, theirs was a hopeless and forbidden love. Mostly they made do with admiring each other from afar, but once or twice they managed to arrange to meet in secret. When they did, they spoke to each other breathlessly and held hands, nothing more. Izabella laughed at how sheltered she had been in those days. Chaperoned almost everywhere, with the thought of actually kissing a boy so far beyond her imagination it hadn't occurred to her to push the boundaries of what was and wasn't allowed. She hadn't even owned a lipstick until she was 18. She wondered if the course of her life would have been different if she had been allowed to follow her heart all those years ago. But there were so many 'ifs' along the way that might have led to a completely different life.

Times had, of course, changed. Like her, András had little regard for his religion now. Any god, however He was worshipped, clearly took no interest in the plight of Hungarians, rich, poor, Catholic or Jew. Instead, András played cards and drank vodka with the local priest and ribbed the poor chap about the not-so-secret girlfriend he regularly visited in town. In turn the Father would ask this good Catholic boy why he never saw him at mass. But the two men shared a common enemy, which they discussed when putting the world to rights over their late-night drinks. They both hated the Communist party for what it had done and what it was still doing, what it had taken from them both and how it treated those that did not agree with its absolute doctrines.

And now Izabella and the balding András were together again after all these years apart. He had never married and Izabella liked to believe it was because he had waited for her, although he could never have predicted the events that had occurred between then and now. How the country they had loved had suffered, and how some of its people had, too. Was András perhaps pleased when he discovered she had been widowed, Izabella wondered? Widowed twice over. Even she struggled to believe that.

And András was also willing, happy even, to take her two children on as his own. Having had a caring stepfather himself, it was a role he was confident in. He had already proved he was good with the siblings, cracking jokes and encouraging them to do their chores around the house by making it into a game. Izabella felt confident that András would do anything for her. He'd even offered to formally adopt Gyorgy and Marta, too, so that their Jewish surname could no longer be held against them. He knew that the kids in Kistelek regularly taunted Izabella's children because of their ethnicity, the hatred the Germans had stoked would take generations to extinguish. Perhaps it would never really go. Now Izabella was hated for other reasons too because of the communists.

And what a welcome András's family had given her and her children when they'd started to court. Farmers were used to rising with the sun, going without and getting things done. Not that farming was the certain life it had once been. By the end of the 1940s over a million people lived on Hungary's farms, but the regime had taken the land and created 'collectives'. András even had cousins who had abandoned the land altogether and moved into town; one was now a pastry chef in Szeged. The war, and more so what came after, had changed everything though and András's humble background and lack of formal education didn't deter Izabella. There was no time for misplaced snobbery among citizens when you lived under a government like theirs.

Life had been no bed of roses for András and his fellow farmers in the years they were apart. Hungarian authorities had ceaselessly tried to incorporate ethnic Hungarian areas in neighbouring countries back into the nation, and courted the Axis powers of Germany, Italy and Japan as it tousled with the Soviets and Yugoslavia. When the war came proper, András was conscripted into the army. But Hungary had sacrificed too much in its attempt to expand its land. By the end of the war and Hungary's surrender, approximately three hundred thousand Hungarian soldiers were dead, Hungary's borders were returned to their pre-1938 lines and the Soviets were effectively in charge. The authorities went on to become little more than a Stalinist servant, sacrificing private enterprise and disrupting the country's whole way of life. And particularly the lives of those that worked the land that had been in their family for generations.

After the war, the life of the Hungarian farmer became a battle in itself. The Rákosi regime had a plan for the people, and supposedly wanted a workers' state, but instead the people were expected to work harder for less. Families were told to turn over their land so that larger state-run operations with their ever-increasing output targets could flourish. Except they didn't. Nothing and nobody flourished, except those at the very top. Displaced farmworkers headed off to industrial jobs they neither wanted nor understood. Now the people were poorer than ever and couldn't use the skills and knowledge handed down by their forefathers. Instead, everyone worked hard to cheat the system, taking a little on the side, hiding some of the livestock and produce, using their wits to ensure they didn't go to bed starving. When the inspectors came to take what was owed, friends had been forewarned and the milk had been diluted.

Even having an opinion on the failures of the regime became dangerous, too. It wasn't unusual to see those that voiced a different opinion beaten unconscious in the street and taken to the fountain at the crossroads to be revived, so they could be beaten again or arrested. The authorities made sure any insubordination was put down and that official political opposition was dispensed with. In 1948 the Russians even had the cheek to call elections with just one candidate to ensure communism was the only 'option'.

It was then that András couldn't keep his frustration to himself anymore, and spoke up about the lack of democracy. In the end, András was taken to court for activities against the state. When Lajos died, András had only recently been released from prison. Perfect timing you might say, thought Izabella. Maybe there was a small part of that foolishly romantic girl within her still that believed in the path of true love after all.

While their relationship was romantic and passionate, Izabella would be lying if she had not accepted that becoming a wife again was essential to her survival. Her home had been taken and her business nationalised. She was effectively banned from working herself because of her supposed status and with Lajos dead and gone, she had no means to support herself and her children. Call it a twist of fate, or a happy coincidence, reconnecting with András had saved her and her family from being homeless and hungry once more.

Izabella had known true starvation in Auschwitz, of course, and the taste was bitter. She didn't want her children to experience that. As a farmer, András, and his family, were never short of food despite the hardships communism had bought. They had plentiful peach trees on the piece of land the family had been allowed to keep for themselves, with strawberries growing under the heavy boughs, too. Gyorgy and Marta loved to help pick the fruit, returning with telltale juice stains around their smiling faces. And just maybe they sampled the melons from the neighbouring farm, too.

She'd had to quiet her mother's objections, of course. She'd always thought András, as a peasant that lived on the land, was somewhat beneath her daughter and he was brought up as a Catholic rather than a Jew. Having left school so early, he wasn't well educated in the formal sense and yet, Izabella told her mother, he was well read, having ploughed through all the classics and taught himself history. He'd also learnt arithmetic through practical use rather than from a book, enough to get a job as an accountant when the government made farming impossible. How could you not admire a man like that?

But her mother warned her that András was a troublemaker, and too keen to vocalise his dislike for the communists. She told Izabella that while she understood that after generations of working the land having it all taken away by the regime gave the farmers a right to be angry, she also said you also needed to know when to keep your opinions to yourself. In fact, his big mouth had got him into trouble already, her mother argued. Heaven knows, the family didn't need to draw any more attention to itself, she'd warned. But for Izabella, András's outspoken nature showed he was passionate and principled. Maybe Hungary needed more men just like that?

Anyway, Izabella had reasoned with her mother, realistically what were the alternatives now? Without a penny to her name, no capacity to work and two children to feed, Izabella was not the marriage prospect she once was. As a non-Jew, András had not the same lived experience of the war as her and her mother, he had not been persecuted simply for existing, so it was harder for him to understand how to contain himself so that he did not antagonise those above him. Perhaps he had not witnessed first-hand the cruelty a man could inflict upon another. Or perhaps inside prison he had? They would share such dark secrets once they were married.

But Izabella knew her mother was still uneasy. She warned her daughter that she had a tendency to jump in headfirst. Would her love for András put her at risk again, thought Izabella?

She would come to learn that ignoring her husband's outspoken past was indeed foolhardy.

Chapter 7

Izabella, 1952, Kistelek

Izabella looked out into the communal yard from the living room window. Her children were happily playing beneath the horse chestnut tree, as they so often were. They sat at its base, backs against the dark scaly bark of the huge trunk, protected by the large canopy of yellowing leaves spreading out above them, playing happily in the sandpit her husband had made there.

This giant guardian had supported the family silently through the years, but how would they manage now she wondered. Who would watch over her and her children when their father was gone?

Izabella knew the seasonal cycle of this tree better than anyone. It flowered in May; with pretty upright white to yellow-red clusters that she liked to think of as spring candles lighting the way to the warmer weather. Then throughout the summer her children could sit shaded by the many branches of its broad and low crown, tentatively learning to swing and hang on the first few boughs. Its spiky, green capsules would begin to form then, too, hinting at the shiny treasures that grew inside. All the local children knew that a game of schoolyard conkers would not be too far away.

In autumn the serrated leaves of the long petiole turned gradually from bright green to yellow then brown, curling at the edges as they did so. The large foliage always looked to her like the palm of a hand stretching out its leaflet fingers, extending a welcome, beckoning them to come and sit for a while. Frequently the whole family, and the neighbours, too, would gladly rest a while by their common, but far from ordinary, ally.

Then, when the leaves finally fell away, a distinctive horseshoe-shaped scar would be left behind on each of the light brown twigs. The fruits would finally fall in the autumn, too, if they survived the poking from the sticks of eager neighbourhood children that was. And as each pericarp hit the ground it shattered to release the glossy mahogany conker stashed within. Delighted children would scoop up the bounty, leaving with stuffed pockets and smiling faces.

To many in Kistelek, this tree wouldn't have seemed unique, of course. There were so many similar trees in the village and it was common to see local children enjoying the glut of conkers in the autumn. And that was exactly why it had held its secret so well. To the Seilers alone this particular tree was very special indeed, and it was deeply rooted in the family's survival and recovery.

Izabella's thoughts turned to her sick husband. He had been ill non-stop for so many months now. His breathing hadn't improved, and she wondered how much longer his weak heart could hold out. As if it wasn't enough that Lajos had been made to suffer in the labour camps, years later he was still paying the price and facing the consequences of the neglect and poor sanitation that his captors had allowed, probably encouraged. Jews after all were expendable to some, she had witnessed that with her own eyes. And like so many of their people held and tortured in the concentration and work camps, lice-born typhus had wreaked havoc on Lajos's body, forever damaging his organs and weakening his ability to fight off infections when they came. Despite his first survival, he had been damaged to the very core, making living after the war another challenge. One he was determined to face down.

Lajos had always been such a hard worker; a credit to the community, and he had deserved so much more she reasoned. His family had kept many businesses running in the village, and rented out houses, too. What would Kistelek have been without the Seilers before the war? Speaking Hungarian, English and German, Lajos had listened to radio broadcasts from across the world avidly. He was also an intelligent man, which is exactly why the family was able to sit and enjoy their yard now, like the children were doing today.

Clever Lajos had understood that dangerous changes were coming when Miklós Kállay was deposed in 1944. Döme Sztójay, who had served as Hungarian ambassador to Germany, replaced Kállay and this new Prime Minister had strong ties with the Third Reich, supporting many German policies. Under Sztójay's premiership the far-right Arrow Cross Party with its leader Ferenc Szálasi was quickly legalised, Hungarian troops were sent to the Eastern Front, political opponents and activists jailed and the nation's Jews deported. Jewish men in the army were no longer soldiers but forced labour, set to the hardest tasks others couldn't and wouldn't do. Captive Jews had no choice, of course, unless they wanted to be beaten to death or shot. Lajos realised he would be targeted and that he had to prepare for the future. He was also concerned that the police and army would soon come to collect anything of value from their family home. And he was right about that too, of course.

As business partners, Lajos had discussed the political climate and its implications with his mother. Like many of her generation though, she thought the troubles would pass. She thought it was enough that she had given many of her precious belongings to neighbours for 'safe keeping' rather than risk them being taken. She also trusted that if she were taken to a ghetto, it would be temporary and that she would return home later to pick up where she left off. Lajos was not as naive and finally convinced her that they should buy some gold for the future. His plan was to then hide it where the authorities would never find it. It was an insurance policy. And one that paid dividends.

When Izabella had first begun working for Lajos it was clear he had returned to nothing after the war. What the authorities had left, looters had taken from his home and business, damaging anything that got in their way or that they didn't need. The borrowed clothes and shoes he wore were ill fitting, his mother was gone and his own health shockingly poor. And yet despite the disappointment of losing everything and the horror that he had witnessed, he was always looking to the future. For Izabella this was compelling. She had wondered how every morning Lajos got up off the bare floorboards he now slept on in place of his bed with a plan of how to reclaim his life. And found the energy to put the plan into practice. It was the attitude she had chosen, too.

And it wasn't too long before she found out about the tree that stood in the yard and the secret it held. A secret kept safe throughout the years of turmoil. Buried beneath the dusty soil at the base of the chestnut tree was a small cache of gold.

Lajos often told Izabella how in his darkest days of labour he had taken comfort in knowing if he could only stay alive long enough to make it back to Kistelek, he would be able to rebuild his life because of what he had hidden. While he waited, he explained to his wide-eyed wife, he had read and re-read the thirty letters he had received from his family for comfort. Throughout his time at the camp he had concealed the papers within his shirt, finally bringing this delicate treasure home. These letters became his comfort when he discovered that his mother, and many of the Jewish villagers, would never return. Izabella marvelled at both Lajos's foresight during the time of chaos before the war and at his resilience as he toiled on the road and railways. Waiting to return. Waiting to restore his family's name and place in village life.

And as Lajos used the buried treasure to rebuild his life, Izabella found she was also impressed by his self-control, unearthing only a tiny piece of the ore at a time and spending it frugally on necessities rather than the luxuries of his former life he surely missed. At first he sold just a little gold in Szeged, and bought stock for his shop. While money became worthless with each passing day, gold had kept its value. In this way, Lajos cheated the hyperinflation Hungary suffered after the war. With the cash he'd raised, Lajos bought the commercial supplies and sold them on at a profit, increasing his own business's cash flow. After that, he rationed out the gold, planning how to make it last as long as possible. Indeed, the very last of this precious resource was not used until

1947, when she was pregnant with Marta and the couple had travelled to Budapest's black market to buy all that the baby needed there.

Perhaps he had learnt the hard way, knowing that a starved prisoner suddenly attending a feast mustn't gorge on the spread. To do so would be to risk your longer-term health. Instead, just as he had been forced to build up his appetite slowly after his labour camp days to avoid further stomach ulcers, he learnt to control any urge to spend and enjoy the gold all at once. And in return for his measured approach he was able to rebuild his life slowly, giving him time to recover both physically and emotionally. This is how he had become her Lajos, a patient, determined, clever man and a practical and loving husband and father.

They hadn't kept the secret alone, however. The Kiss family that lived across the yard had first rented their home from Lajos in the 1930s. With a mirror-image house and an identical window that also looked out onto the yard, it was impossible to believe the family had not seen Lajos bury the gold beneath the tree. But they did not ask about what was being buried; and, for their own safety, Lajos did not tell them either.

Lajos Kiss and his wife, Sara, were devout Catholics. They brought up their five children with love, and went to mass twice a day, every day. The family was not driven by the ever-changing circumstances or the politics of man. They listened only to the teachings of Christianity. They did not judge the Seilers for being Jewish either, they knew it was not their right to steal or kill based on prejudice. When the Jewish villagers had been held in the ghetto, the Kiss family had taken milk and medicines to them, risking their own safety for no other reason than to do what was right. They also looked after their neighbours as much as they could through the troubled times, and said nothing about the tree and the possibility of its treasure to those that asked. For surely they had been asked many times for any secrets their Jewish neighbours held.

The Kiss family ran the only pharmacy in the area. The dispensary, just like the shop of their neighbour landlords, was at the front of the house.

Lajos Kiss was tall and slim, and always had a smile on his face. His wife was the opposite shape, but just as cheerful. The couple stood each day in their white coats among the meticulously labelled dark wooden shelves with their rows of glass bottles. They were always ready to help, advise and mix up medicines from scratch. Serving the whole community, regardless of their race or religion, they applied the discretion and empathy that was an essential part of their professional lives into their everyday behaviour.

In time Izabella had become close to Sara and her Lajos, too. Their children played together under the tree, the older Kiss boys climbing up the boughs easily. When Sara's sister came to live in the third bedroom with a view out onto the yard, the children quickly learnt to call her 'Auntie Danci', a reference to her earlier career aspirations. Now whenever Izabella cooked or baked, an extra portion would be made for the kindly neighbours. Sara was a terrible cook by her own admission and Izabella loved to share a hearty meal or a delicious treat. It was the least she could do.

So much went on in the yard but it was always kept clean and tidy. Apart from the horse chestnut, no other flowers or trees made their home there. At the back was the storage unit for their building supplies business. All day, people would come and go, delivering more items or collecting others. When it was sunny, the sunshine would be constant, which made it ideal for wash days, when Izabella and Franciska, who came to help her run the house, used the open space to clean the linens before hanging them to dry in the heat of the loft. Later they would be ironed and starched, so that everything was stiff and orderly. Izabella loved clean linen.

It was also perfect for the hard work of making *tarhonya*. Franciska, who minded the children when Izabella was occupied with the business, made the traditional pasta here. While her teenage daughter, Piri, played with the children, Franciska would hand mix flour, salt and eggs in large wooden containers, making a stiff mixture that would then be formed into the rice-sized pellets. These would then be laid out on covered tables to dry in the sun. When it was finished, the *tarhonya* would be hung in 2kg cotton sacks and stored in the larder, ready for the families to consume that year. When sautéed and boiled the pasta was a satisfying side to traditional dishes such as paprika chicken and Franciska was well known locally for her *tarhonya* skills.

Izabella's thoughts returned to her current predicament. She had a business to run, a home to mind and Marta and Gyorgy, who was already showing his father's determination. Her children were so young and blissfully unaware of how hard life could become in the blink of an eye. How would their father's death affect them?

Izabella realised it was her turn to be resilient now. Her own treasure sat beneath the chestnut tree. Was it as safe as the gold had been all those years before, she wondered?

Marta was sad to learn that the chestnut tree was recently cut down to make way for housing. Looking back, she remembers many family jokes about the tree's secret, although she was often too young to understand them.

Chapter 8

Marta, 1972, Temple Fortune

Sitting at her desk, ready to write about her mother's passing to those that did not already know, Marta pressed the middle fingers of her left hand over the lower part of her forehead and moved them to massage her left temple. Thinking back to 1965 when she first left for England, Marta reheard the words her mother had whispered into her ear as they stood at that bus stop. The message had been clear, of course, even though it had been easy to ignore at the time.

Marta thought back to that long journey, and how she had felt arriving in a foreign country. It had certainly taken her a few days to settle into her new lifestyle. At the end of her journey to London, Aranka had actually found Marta fast asleep on the train seat; her niece so utterly exhausted she hadn't even woken up upon arrival.

Luckily Marta had found herself a window seat, and Aranka could spot her as she raced up and down the platform wondering where her charge was. Marta shuddered remembering how she had suffered with travel sickness for most of the journey, firstly on the bus as her seat was facing the back and especially as she crossed the Channel. With limited food and sleep over the days of travelling, it wasn't surprising that she had fallen into a deep sleep.

The next day, however, barely recovered, Marta toured the city by double-decker bus with her aunt. Up on the top deck, London seemed to her simply a blur of unfathomable lights.

She remembered that, thinking that her aunt's successful business in England meant they were rich, her mother had hoped that Aranka could easily afford a new coat for Marta once the winter came. Accordingly, Marta's suitcase held just summer clothes. It wasn't too long before her aunt discovered what the relatives that were eking out an existence in communist Hungary expected of her.

But things weren't as grand for Aranka as her family had imagined Marta found. By the mid-1960s fashions had changed and mass-produced items were hitting the market, meaning the hat business was not as buoyant as it had been. Aranka was also struggling with arthritic fingers, needing Marta's help to complete her work. Although back in Kistelek, the family regarded Aranka as fortunate because she had escaped the wave of fascism that swept over their homelands, Marta's aunt was only able to get by because Harold Wilson's rent controls in England had kept the outgoings for her well-placed flat so low. Later, she had lived off a small pension from the German government that acted as compensation for her wartime displacement.

Despite this relative hardship, Marta's aunt paid for her niece's school, travel and food, and even gave her 10 shillings a week pocket money. But Aranka made it quite clear to Marta that if she wanted to follow the trend and smoke, which Marta really did, then the cigarettes would have to be paid for with her pocket money. And in the end, Marta even received a very fine coat indeed through her aunt's fashion industry contacts.

Marta had always appreciated her aunt's generosity, but by the January she had been keen to earn a little extra spending money, so she became a 'teatime girl', helping out a local family for the two hours around their evening meal. Helping with the cooking and washing up, the job gave her enough cash to buy fashionable shoes, despite her aunt's reservations about Marta taking a job while she was on a student visa. Marta found she was more than capable at the role having always helped her mother at home and having spent so much time caring for Laci.

Looking back now, Marta saw that without really realising it, within six months of living in England she had decided she didn't ever want to go back to Hungary. She had been desperately in love with a young man called Paul. He was studying economics at Manchester University and had plans to become a political journalist. Unfortunately his parents thought he was too young for a long-term relationship and broke up the romance. Instead, Marta found herself dating Peter, who was a hairdresser in Baker Street. He had a Hungarian background, although he'd come to the UK when he was 14. But, with Marta's studies finishing, her time in England was coming to an end. Perhaps that's why Marta readily accepted when he asked her to marry him, despite knowing he was not 'the one' of whom young girls usually dream. Much later, Paul returned to tell Marta he couldn't live without her, and suggested they start a new life together in Israel. But it was too late; Marta had made her choice and planned to make her marriage work.

Marta then found that since she was married to an English national, the Home Office extended her visa allowing her to stay in England. Later she stood in amusement as a civil servant inspected the couple's rooms to check they really did live together as husband and wife. Taking note of the male clothes hung in the wardrobe in their home in Chalk Farm, the Home Office representative was satisfied this was a real marriage. Now Marta could relax into her new life and country, and look for work proper.

Perhaps with her parents' background as village shopkeepers, and her aunt also a small business owner, it was inevitable Marta would pick a retail career of some sort; it seemed all her family knew just how to get a sale going. It was, in fact, also a practical decision, since, after receiving the letter telling her she was now able to legally work, when Marta scanned a copy of the *Evening News*, it seemed to her that she wasn't qualified for anything but retail.

When she started at John Bell and Croydon in Wigmore Street, selling mobility aids, she quickly earned a promotion. Marta had been proud that she had proved she had the family gift, too, but what she really wanted was to follow in her aunt's stylish footsteps and move into fashion. Her desire led her to an opportunity at Fenwick in Bond Street.

With a husband and a career she loved, Marta really had begun the new, safer and happier life her mother had wanted for her all along. It must have brought Izabella much relief to know that her daughter would not be hounded for her race or punished for her hard work and success, thought Marta.

While Marta was forging her new life England, her parents moved to Budapest by way of a permitted house swap. Marta imagined that the appeal of this new big city was that no one cared if you were a 'proper' communist and agreed with the government or not, or even if you were a Jew or had chosen to marry one. In Kistelek, she realised, everyone had known everyone else's business and Izabella had found it hard when she had returned from Auschwitz and saw so much prejudice still existed. If the family weren't being despised because they were Jewish, Marta's mother was being penalised for her supposed Bourgeois background and for marrying a man that spoke out against communism. After years of fighting such bigotry, Izabella had clearly had enough. Anonymity in the city must have been a blessed relief for her mother, thought Marta. Izabella would have been able to walk down the street to the market without glancing sideways to see who was looking at or gossiping about her. And hopefully, she no longer felt the constant need to keep her wits about her, or live with the fear that she would feel a hand fall heavily on her shoulder.

Throughout her time in England, Marta had been keeping in touch with her friends and family by letter, but when the Hungarian authorities realised their comrade hadn't come back, they had insisted Marta's parents write to her and first beg, and later demand, that she come home. Now that she had begun to understand that her homeland was not as she had once seen it, and feeling it was for the best, Marta deliberately had less contact with those left back in Hungary for a few years.

She did this to protect those she cared about as nobody could risk being associated with a 'traitor' to the state. Marta now knew those she loved might be in danger because of their friendship with her. From the freedom of England it became harder and harder to believe the regime in Hungary operated through fear and intimidation and that she had only just recognised this. The people were virtual prisoners in their own country, she had realised. It was impossible to believe that she too had lived like that, and even supported the Young Communist Party as well. Brainwashing really was the word for it. Oh how her stepfather would smile to see she had changed her views! She'd lost count of the good-humoured but passionate political arguments she'd had with András over the years.

Many years later Marta's mother had managed to make it out of Hungary to visit her in Temple Fortune, staying for just over a week. Marta remembers how she hurriedly arranged for Izabella to see a Hungarian-speaking private doctor during the trip, as she had been so ill for so long but the doctors she saw in Hungary hadn't been able to find a reason for her deteriorating health. After listening to her life story and examining her, the English doctor had no firm diagnosis either, but he'd also said he wasn't surprised she didn't feel well considering how she had suffered years of starvation and stress. Marta was now always looking at the world she thought she knew from a different angle. Why had her mother never talked about these hardships, she'd wondered at the time.

But by 1972, back in Hungary, Izabella was found to have bowel cancer and her colon was removed to try and halt the spread of the disease. When her bowels were reconnected and her health deteriorated further, András had written to Marta explaining just how ill her mother now was. This left Marta with a dilemma; she wasn't keen on returning to the country she had abandoned but she knew her mother's health was fading and that she needed to see her.

Using her British passport, Marta had applied for a visa to Hungary, hoping she would pass undetected through the country's border. She wanted to be an insignificant British tourist, not a dissident sneaking back to see those she loved. Marta knew the Hungarian authorities didn't take kindly to those that had shown them up internationally.

In the end, Marta made it to Budapest without any problems and managed to see her mother in hospital every day. Seeing how cumbersome her colostomy bag was, she'd been determined to find a better alternative once she was back in the UK.

But leaving at the end of her stay had not been a pleasant experience. Stopped in passport control, a surly officer informed Marta she should never have been allowed a visa to enter the country but waved her on regardless. As Marta sat in the departure lounge, she felt the dread that had been so familiar to her family, her mouth dry and her heart racing. She sat with her right leg crossed over her left as she waited for her flight to be called, her knee bouncing up and down. Only when the plane was finally in the air could her breathing return to normal.

It had been a week later that Marta had received the call from András to tell her that her mother had died.

After her previous nerve-wracking airport experience, Marta decided she wasn't going to put herself at any risk this time. She reapplied for a visa but this time it was denied and she was instead invited to see the Hungarian ambassador. It seemed that the authorities had caught up on exactly who she was now! The ambassador was understanding of her predicament and advised that she ask the Hungarian government to remove her citizenship entirely instead. She agreed.

She knew the only safe way to visit Hungary now was to go as a British citizen, with the protection that offered her. But Marta's request to no longer be a Hungarian national was dealt with slowly and in the end granted too late for her mother's funeral. The Hungarian government and its political machinations had prevented her from saying a final goodbye to her mother. It seemed then that the callous regime of her home was omnipotent in both Izabella's life and death. Izabella had been persecuted even at the end.

For Marta this was the moment she realised the sacrifice her mother had made when she left for England on that warm September dawn a decade earlier. In the mindset of the carefree young girl she was, Marta imagined she was just heading off for a stopgap trip until she would return home to study in the country she had never yet left and perhaps understood even less.

But for Izabella it had been so much more, it was the gift of freedom she was finally giving to her daughter, via a relative that had been able to escape many of the horrors those left behind had faced. By encouraging Marta to leave both her and Hungary behind, Izabella was giving her daughter a chance at a life and a future she was never able to have herself as a Jewish Hungarian in her home nation.

For Izabella, Hungary was not a safe place and she could not rest until her daughter was not at risk there. It dawned on Marta that her mother had never felt welcome in her own birthplace; she had been abused, excluded, taken, tortured, starved, robbed, punished and controlled. Izabella had not lived her life in Hungary but, rather, survived it.

And Marta had begun to understand what it is to be both a survivor, and also, the child of a survivor.

Chapter 9

Lajos, 1944, Sopron

It had been a long time since his very last pair of socks had worn through, leaving his ill-fitting boots to rub his protruding anklebone raw again and again as he worked. But Lajos had become so used to discomfort. He barely felt pain anymore as he followed the orders barked at him for hours on end, from first light until it was too late to see the road he was digging in front of him. His task now was simply to be able to bear each day as well as he could, alongside his camp brothers, who had until last month been in the village of Csenger, by the banks of the river Szamos. The men, united as much by their Jewishness as their forced labour, toiled together in the hope of one day being free. Whatever freedom now meant for a Jewish man in the German-occupied Hungary.

Initially, many men of age had been called up to the country's army and given a uniform. However, those that were Jewish received a shovel rather than a gun with which to serve. The Horthy Regime considered Jews, as they did all political dissenters and ethnic minorities, a threat to national security that would not be tolerated, and in an ideal world disposed of. Once it had used up any resources that could be extracted from them first, of course. After all, even healthy Jewish men could work. In 1939 it had taken care to put in place a National Defence Act that ensured any 'undesirable' military personnel could be 'deployed' to build roads, drain swamps and perform 'earthworks'. Just a few years later all pre-existing Jewish army officers were stripped of their rank and sent instead to labour camps too. Their uniform was taken, too, and by 1942 a simple yellow armband over civilian clothes declared them a Jew, and nothing more.

And so it was that from 1942 Lajos had been sent every year to work at a labour camp for several months at a time, returning home in between these periods. Sometimes his group worked on railways, other times on farms. To begin with the men were moved by train and lived in requisitioned Jewish houses. As he was able to stay in touch with his home, his family and their businesses, the situation seemed acceptable despite the fact he had not chosen to support the war and worried more and more about the direction the government was taking as it allied itself to Germany.

Then the atmosphere changed. Increasing prejudice meant that any pretence that Jews were equal members of Hungarian society was dropped and conditions in the camps deteriorated rapidly. Those in charge were able to inflict beatings, docking of rations and even executions, as they saw fit. The physical demands on camp workers became more and more gruelling, supplies dwindled and conscripts, now unable to leave the camps at all, found they were still dressed in their inadequate summer clothing despite the onset of the bitter winter. Jewish workers mattered so little they were marched through minefields to clear them for troops. Now the labourers were less low-grade army personnel and more prisoners. The soldiers in charge carried weapons, and became guards rather than brothers in arms. Now when they were moved to their next job they marched on foot, and considered themselves lucky if they got to sleep in open cattle wagons.

Lajos knew he had fared better than some of his Jewish countrymen, however; those that were too young or too old to work, for example. He had heard they had been gathered up and sent elsewhere. There were stories of what had happened, too terrible to comprehend. Later he would learn that barely existing in a labour camp had spared him, and many others, from the gas chambers. However, it wasn't hard for him to also understand how some work units were wiped out through sheer brutality and neglect, while others had as few as 5 per cent of their members survive. Forty thousand Hungarian Jews were killed in the *Munkaszolgálat*, the Jewish forced-labour service that pre-dated the German occupation.

Now it was July 1944 and German soldiers were in charge of the camp. Lajos was a long way from home, first in a part of Hungary that had at one time been Romanian and now, further north in Sopron, close to the Austrian border. The ever-shifting borders of Hungary and its neighbours always came with a personal cost, he thought. Would being marched here in freezing conditions cost him his leg, he wondered. it was covered in frostbite and in desperate need of medical attention.

He was also a long way from his dear mother, her letters and parcels no longer reaching him, the last received back in Csenger. Cecilia Lovi sent her son desperately needed essentials such as soap and underwear, and often a traditional poppy seed cake. He had shared what was sent in the parcels with the others, as that was the way to survive the harsh conditions, working as a close team against their captors. Some of the men he knew from his village, as they were called up together, others he had become close to at the camp. They were all Jewish and their survival became dependent on this ability to work together. It was interesting that war pulled people apart, but also together. What was the stronger emotion Lajos wondered, love or hate?

When one of the group made a plan to escape, he decided not to join him. He knew his leg was weak and he didn't want to hold back Matyi, who was headed to Balf via Kapuvár, where he hoped to reunite with his daughter. Instead he promised he would write to his camp mate's family as soon as he could, to tell them what had happened. He wondered if Matyi would make it out and be reunited with his loved ones. The fact that his friend seemed to have got away so far was positive thought Lajos; perhaps the guards were more worried about retreating from the Red Army than counting prisoners right now. If there was a chance he would be left unheeded, maybe he could make it across the border and find a doctor. Although he was just as likely to be shot by his captors; they wouldn't like the Russians to free us, he realised.

The letters he received from his mother were not for sharing with anyone. They were precious and his to cherish alone. He kept them, bundled together and hidden in his shirt, compressing the whitish-yellow paper stack over time. He made sure to never leave them out and visible in case a vindictive guard chose to destroy them for fun. They were his lifeline. He vowed to keep them safe until he could return home and place them in his desk.

His mother's letters were not always good news, of course, because what good news was there? Yet when he was able to reply he took care to make light of his own conditions in an attempt to ease his mother's burden. Instead of telling her he was starved and sick with typhus, he thanked her for what she sent and tried to reassure her that things would be okay, despite the fact he felt very much to the contrary.

Lajos knew he was his mother's confidante, their closeness cemented through years of living and working together, his father and stepfather having both died, leaving his mother without a partner to share her life with. He knew his mother had been strong for the family then, running several businesses alongside one other, leading the local trade association and regularly being listed as one of the top tax payers in the area. His sister, Aranka, older than him by three years, had married and left the family home but he had remained single, unable to find a woman he was happy to share his life with, one that could measure up to the formidable yet tender woman his mother was. He wondered if he ever would.

He had learnt so much from his mother, his own business acumen garnered as a result of watching and working with her over the years. The elders were respected in their community and he had been happy to defer to her over many decisions that affected both their professional and personal life. But the older generation had also been naive to believe that the future would be bright for Hungarian Jews and that the place where they had built their lives was safe and welcoming. His mother was happy with her businesses and the social life that revolved around the synagogue and its community. She didn't have the

Cecilia Lovi, 1877–44.

Cecilia Lovi outside the pharmacy the Seilers rented to the Kiss family.

Lajos Seiler, 1904–52.

Izabella Seiler (née Furedi), 1919–73.

Aranka Weiss (née Seiler), 1901–92.

Izabella in Belsen with friends she made after liberation, 1945. The British soldier that asked her to return home with him is marked.

Marta Seiler on her father Lajos's
knee, 1947.

The Seiler family, Izabella, Gyorgy, Marta and Lajos, 1949.

András Barkanyi with Izabella, Marta, Gorgy (top right) and Laszlo (bottom right), 1962.

Marta and Gyorgy pose outside their house near the chestnut tree, 1965.

Marta and her brothers with András, 1975.

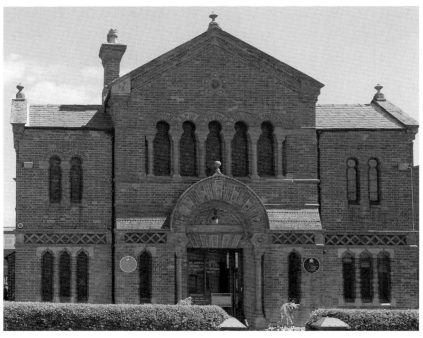

The former synagogue in Cheetham Hill that is now home to Manchester Jewish Museum. (With thanks to Manchester Jewish Museum)

HRH Queen Elizabeth II visiting Manchester Jewish Museum on her Golden Jubilee Tour, 2002. (With thanks to Manchester Jewish Museum)

Gyorgy Seiler by the woods in Israel that
he dedicated to his and Marta's stepfather,
András, after his death.

The Seiler shop in Kistelek as it is being demolished to make way for new
housing, 2021.

Kistelek train station. (Beroesz via Wikimedia Commons)

Kistelek, with the Saint Stephen of Hungary church in view. (Tibi Csoki via Wikimedia Commons)

In one of Cecilia's letters to Lajos, she writes about a lack of food and wood and says she has registered her house with the authorities as she was required to do.

Cecilia writes from the ghetto to Lajos at his labour camp, explaining how crowded her accommodation is.

Kistelek 1945 szept.20

Drága jó Testvérem,Sógorom !

Sokáig töprengtem irjak-ne irjak,vajjon megkapjátok-e levelemet,egy pár vöröskeresztes üzenetet már küldtem,még eddig semmi válasz. Kezdek nagyon nyugtalankodni miattatok. Érthető,már senkim nincs csak Ti vagytok,ragaszkodom Hozzátok. De remélhetőleg csak a körülmények akadályozták meg hogy rendszeresen hirt kapjunk,ill.kapjak Tőletek. Sajnos ugy látszik ami engem illet a többesszámról le kell szoknom. Legutoljára 1944 januárjában /kb./ kaptunk levelet Tőletek fotókkal együtt. El sem képzelitek mekkora örömet jelentett az nekünk de azóta semmi,mégis ugy érzem hogy Ti teljesen jól vagytok,eltekintve persze a lelkiektől mi miattunk,ami -sajnos- nem is volt indokolatlan.

A legdrágább Anya a mi Anyuskánk nem tért haza a deportálásból.Óráról órára csökken a remény hogy még egyszer megcsókolhatom szelid párnás kezét. Azok sem tértek vissza akikkel együtt volt -fiatalabbak nála. A 2 Schréger lár volt mellette a gettóban és később a vagonban. Nem jöttek ők sem haza. Nagyon messzire nem kerülhetett Szegény,mert az ő drága szive olyan gyenge volt hogy nem birhatta sokáig a vagonutazást ahol 80-at préseltek össze egy kocsiban. Én XX 1944 febr.24-én bevonultam munkatáborba,ahová csak egy-egy levelet irhatott. Májusban beszoritották az egész zsidó lakosságot a Mathézer féle fatelepre,ill.annak lakásába. Akinek nem jutott hely az a padláson aludt. Képzel Aranyom azt a zsufoltságot a lakásban,Drágánk egy órát sem aludt egész idő ala idegei már teljesen tönkrementek,csoda hogy egyáltalán kibirta a gettóéletet. Junius 1?-án vitték először Szegedre vagonban,aztán tovább a szomoru uton.

Én ma már jól vagyok,eltekintve természetesen attól hogy semmim nincs. Május közepén értem haza,teljesen kifosztott lakásba. Egyetlen zsebkendő a szekrényekben nem maradt,egyetlen edény vagy üveg a kamrában,minden eltünt. Butorok egyrésze megvan,persze összekarmolva,összetörve. Siralmas volt a helyzet,azóta már vettem 1-2 inget,egy cipőt és egyetmást. Most már ágyban alszom lepedőn,ami igen nagy dolog. Ez azonban mind semmi ahhoz képest hogy drága jó Anyánk nem jött vissza. Ha minden elveszett volna csak Ő jött volna haza. Április közepén értem Pestre Ausztriából viszontagságos körülmények közt sulyos lázasan,flecktifusszal és tüdőgyulladással. 2 hétig eszméletlenül feküdtem a kórházban,igazán csodának számit hogy élek. 38 kilóval kerültem haza itthon kicsit hirtelen kezdtem táplálkozni és kaptam egy gyomorfekélyt. Amikor a szegedi klinikára beszállitottak gyomorperforáció ugy néztem ki hogy meg sem akartak operálni. Mégis az operáció sikerült,a gyomrot bevarrták aminek most 4 hete. Azóta rohamosan szedem magam össze,ma ismét a régi sulyomnál vagyok és ugyanugy nézek ki mint régebben. Valóban sok mindenen mentem keresztül,különösen egy év óta. Egy levél kerete -még száz levél is- nagyon szük ahhoz hogy az ember elmondhassa milyen volt az élete az utolsó időkben. Remél Aranyom számitsz rá hogy annak idején jöttök haza. Nem szabad kicsinyeskedni sem idővel sem pénzzel. Rájöttünk már mindnyájan mit érnek a guruló aranyak hogy az életben csak az egymás megbecsülése,a szeretet ami érték. Természetesen szándékozom majd megnősülni,mert igy élni nem élet,csak most még nagyon frissek az emlékek drága Anyámról. A mészüzletet élesztgetem több-kevesebb -inkább kevesebb- sikerrel. De valahogy egészen közömbösen érintenek az anyagi dolgok. Tökéletesen megelégszem annyi eredménnyel ami a létfenntartást biztositja. Különben sem célszerü nagy lakást,háztartást vezetni.

Seiler Sándorék /Gyuri kivételével/ hazajöttek. Idusék szintén,a gye rekek is. Lóránték mindkét fiuk még oda van. Szörnyü szerencsétlenség. Az egé Popper család hazajött,igazán szerencsések,csak a Laci nincs itthon,de róla v lami értesülés van. Általában a kistelekieket szerencsésnek mondják más város hoz képest,ugyanis a zsidóknak kb.egy harmada visszakerült. Igy sikerült megtartani az ünnepeket is.

Már jeleztem vöröskeresztes lapon is hogy Adolfék jelentkeztek Shanghaiból. Jól vannak mindhárman,üzlet mozog -azt hiszem étkezde- nagyon szeretnék a Ti cimeteket tudni. Az ő cime : Shanghai C/o Hicem, 66 Ankuo Lu Én nem irtam neki,irjatok Ti az én nevemben is.

Compiled at: BELSEN
Nationality: HUNGARIAN
Date: MAY/JUNE
           1945

NAME		NUMBER	CIVILIAN TRADE
TANNENBAUM	Irene	B/00093697	Household
TARKOVICZ	Tobi	G/01698020	Household
TAUB	Heli		Household
TAUB	Iren	B/00106921	Dressmaker
TAUB	Jolan	G/01697953	Dressmaker
TAUB	Laura	G/01698441	Household
TAUB	Roza	01697609	Dressmaker
TAUB	Sari	01818392	Dressmaker
TAUBER	Isabella	G/01848154	Household
TAUBER	Valeria	B/00119265	Household
TAUBMANN	Ibolya	B/00093670	Student
TAUSZIG	Eva	G/01858328	Hairdresser
TAUSZIG	Olga	G/01858327	
TEBOVICZ	Frida	G/01698276	Household
TEICH	Anna	B/00093716	Dressmaker
TEICH	Rozsi	B/00093717	Dressmaker
TEICH	Serena	B/00093715	Dressmaker
TEICHMANN	Frieda	B/00093703	Dressmaker
TEICHMANN	Roszi	G/01697908	Household
TEICHMANN	Sary	G/01697909	Household
TEITELBAUN	Hainal	00119353	Household
TELLER	Illona	001532170	
TELLER	Piri	001532169	
TENNER	Olga	B/00119020	Dressmaker
TESSLER	Esther	B/00106779	Household
TESSLER	Razi	B/00106778	Household
TESSLER	Rucia		Dentist
TESSLER	Sara	B/00106777	Buyer
TESZELER	Berta	B/00048032	Household
TESZLER	Blima	B/00119408	Chemist
TESZLER	Etelka	G/01848370	Private
TESZLER	Gitta	B/00048031	Household
TESZLER	Ilona	G/01848368	Clerk
TESZLER	Rozsi	G/01848369	Milliner
TINES	Sophie	G/01540598	Household
TOCHAUER	Margit	B/00048169	Clerk
TOCKAJA	Steffi		Dressmaker
ORZS	Rozsi	G/01698300	Household
TOTH	Julianna	G/01698362	Household
TRAUB	Hilde	G/01858158	Dressmaker
TRAUB	Szabina	G/01858337	Nurse
TREBICZ	Gabriella	G/01697940	Milliner
TREBICZ	Helen	G/01697939	Dressmaker
TREMMEL	Juliana	G/01697531	Household
TRONSTEIN	Olga	B/00048055	Dressmaker
TROTZER	Anna	B/00093789	Housekeeper
TSCHESNER	Anna	G/01697814	Dressmaker
TSCHESNER	Hedi	G/01697813	Dressmaker
TSCHESNER	Rosi	G/01697815	Dressmaker
TURTA	Klara	G/01838680	Private
TURTAK	Erszi	G/01838793	Private
TUSAK	Piroska	B/01697533	Household
UHR	Irene	G/01540856	Household
ULTMANN	Iboja	G/01540717	Household
ULTMANN	Ilona	G/01540716	Household
UNGAR	Edit	B/00093799	Dressmaker
UNGAR	Klara	G/01858286	Guide
UNGAR	Livia	G/01697927	Dressmaker
UNGAR	Magda	G/01697928	Milliner
UNGAR	Magda	G/01698304	Dressmaker
UNGAR	Margit	B/00093798	Housekeeper
UNGER	Magda	G/01858329	Household
UNGER	Regina	B/00106782	Household

A record of Izabella's Auschwitz tattoo number. She is listed as 'Isabella Tauber' alongside the number G/01848154.

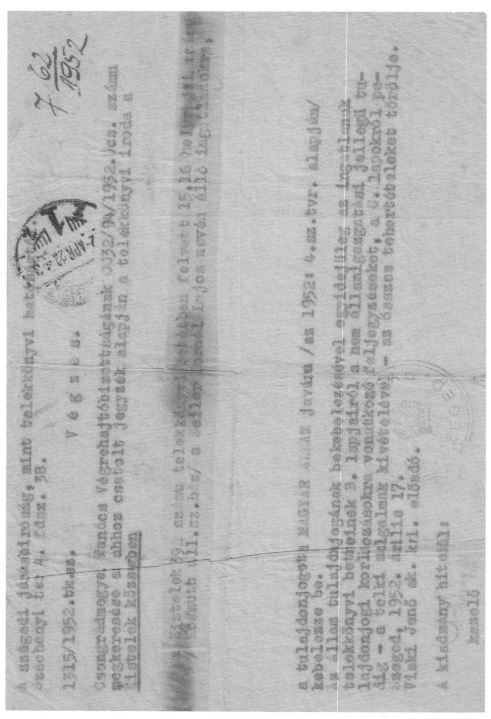

The paperwork Izabella received when the authorities nationalised her home and business, 1952.

Hungarian Jews arrive in Auschwitz from the ghetto, 1944. (Yad Vashem via Wikimedia Commons)

Hungarian Jews arrive in Auschwitz. These women and children have been selected for extermination, 1944. (Yad Vashem via Wikimedia Commons)

Dr Fritz Klein, Bergen–Belsen's camp doctor, stands in a mass grave. Klein was convicted of war crimes and executed, 1945. (No. 5 Army Film & Photographic Unit via Wikimedia Commons)

Three women suffering from typhus lie closely packed together in one of the huts at Bergen-Belsen after liberation, 1945. (No. 5 Army Film & Photographic Unit via Wikimedia Commons)

After the liberation of Bergen-Belsen, German nurses wash an emaciated man at the 'Human Laundry', 1945 (No. 5 Army Film & Photographic Unit via Wikimedia Commons)

An emaciated Hungarian woman after the liberation of Bergen-Belsen, 1945. (No. 5 Army Film & Photographic Unit via Wikimedia Commons)

A tank sits outside a ruined building in Budapest, 1956. (ETH-Bibliothek Zürich via Wikimedia Commons)

A Soviet self-propelled artillery vehicle sits amid buildings damaged after the 1956 uprising in Budapest. (Fortepan via Wikimedia Commons)

inclination to be interested in world politics or to listen to the radio. But he had listened to the news and feared the worst, and now, day by day, his fears were being realised. If only more people had understood what was happening, and acted then. Perhaps all this could have been avoided.

His mother wrote every day if she could. In her letters, she poured out her worries, holding nothing back, and they sat heavy on Lajos's shoulders, a mental anguish to add to his physical struggles. She became increasingly desperate as the war progressed, her tone changing until she was pleading for his strength and support. When the new anti-Semitic laws came into being in March of that year (1944) Jews were no longer allowed money and jewellery, and his mother had described how day after day the authorities came to raid their home and business, taking anything of value, stripping the rooms and the shop store bare. These beasts had taken his typewriter and his radio, and, here at the camp, he was powerless to stop them. He was powerless to protect his mother, too, he realised. And that had always been his role.

Cecilia had been ill the previous year, and was admitted to hospital, not expected to recover. She had defied the odds, however, but now needed constant care to get through the day. Since Jews were no longer allowed to employ people, his mother's helper, who had been with them since she was a child, was told she couldn't stay and work as a carer for the elderly woman. She left the house in floods of tears, as she had no family to go to, and nowhere to live. Without his mother this poor girl would no longer have an income to allow her to rent a room, and wouldn't be able to put food on her plate and clothes on her back. His mother could not remedy the situation, and neither could he. But perhaps this girl would be better off without Jews as friends and employers now anyway. As the girl had left Cecilia had pressed some spare cash into her hand, as worried for the girl as the girl was for her former employer.

Then it was declared that Jews could no longer live alone in houses with more than a certain number of rooms; instead Germans were billeted on their homes. An officer moved into his mother's house on Kossuth Lajos Utca and she was told to take what was left of her things to the one room she was now allowed to live in within her home. In some ways the arrival of this gentleman of rank pleased his mother. She had described her uninvited houseguest as well mannered, and the company meant that she was no longer alone, now that both Lajos and her carer had been lost. Being multi-lingual, Cecilia was able to understand the officer when he spoke German to her and she reported that he treated her well. With his mother's health in decline, Lajos hoped that if this man truly was kind, that he might take pity on his elderly host. Could a German individual be kind to a Jew he wondered, or were they hardwired to be heartless?

But her letters also reminded Lajos of his dear mother's eccentricities, and he especially savoured the words she wrote that showed him that her personality could not be cowed by either poor health or the conditions she found herself in. Cecilia described how she was herded up like an animal and taken to the ghetto by cart, where she was mostly bedridden, complaining about the terrible overcrowding and the distance to the toilet.

Yet he had to smile as she proudly declared her social standing had been acknowledged even here by the fact she shared a mattress with the wife of a Rabbi. Only my mother would care about something like that now, he chuckled to himself. But he was also heartbroken to think his mother was so unwell in such a degrading place. At least the letters also said that two sisters from a family they knew well were taking care of her. It seemed that others knew the way to survive this hell was through fellowship. Labour camp brothers and ghetto families, these bonds were the difference between survival, or its alternative.

His mother's letters were written in pencil on lined paper at first, and then, when that ran out, on the postcards they had had printed for their business, with the family name embossed on the bottom left. The day they chose these cards together seemed like a lifetime away, deciding carefully upon the size and style of the lettering, as if any of that mattered now. Later his mother had to go to the post office to purchase official pre-stamped cards to use to communicate instead, a simple journey for someone that was healthy, but difficult for her when she was frail. By this point, it was clear there was less privacy afforded to any communications, and his mother's tone showed him that she was not able to write freely about her experiences. A red mark on each of these letters showed that someone had 'checked' through them before delivery to ensure nothing was being reported that could be considered subversive. It was clear that any slight misdemeanour could provide an opportunity for further punishment.

He had collected letters from other relatives also; one desperately asked Lajos where her husband could be and why

Lajos was unable to write back to her. If only she knew my position, he thought. His cousin also wrote to him, and later he would head there for safety after the war had ended. Each envelope bore the address of the work camp, etched into the paper, a name and a place that was etched into his brain forever, too. A place he would never forget, even when he tried to.

Lajos thought that perhaps he held onto his letters as a sign of hope. Hope that he would be somewhere safe one day and able to look back upon this bundle of papers as a record of a time that had long since passed. A time that he had survived. The letters had borne witness to the suffering he had endured when he first read them and keeping them meant he had a future beyond today. He had other hope, too. He could see that German soldiers were passing his work camp daily on their way to the Russian Front. If they need to repel the Soviets then Lajos thought that it signified all was not well for the army, he reasoned. Surely liberation could be possible? And all this would be over. Soon, he prayed, soon.

After liberation the letters would bring considerable comfort to Lajos when he learnt of his mother's death, which likely happened on her way to Auschwitz. He would never know for sure how and when she had died of course, but he was heartened by the thought it was probably through ill health rather than violence directed at her. He liked to think she died in her sleep, maybe even on that shared mattress that she so approved of. A tiny piece of comfort in her last moments.

The letters then became a piece of their shared history he could keep forever, a physical reminder of the love and devotion to each other they had experienced. He continued to keep in touch with those close to him by letter after the war too, describing dealing with the sorrow he felt over the loss of his mother as 'like emptying the ocean with a teaspoon'.

His daughter, Marta, would read those letters and discover her family's past.

Chapter 10

Izabella, 1957, Kistelek

'It's him, it's András,' Izabella shouts as she jumps up from her chair, hand half waving in the air. The Sunday mending that was resting in her lap scatters on the ground beneath her. It lays forgotten on the floor as she rushes indoors. Those around her stay rooted to the spot, sensing her panic but not fully understanding the reason for it.

Izabella reappears from the house, 'I saw his face through the window,' she says by way of an explanation, before she rushes into the store room at the back of the house, returning with the black 350 cm3 Dampf-Kraft-Wagen motorcycle András had always used to travel to work. The others see she now has changed clothes, from a skirt into trousers, and that she is hurriedly tying her hair back. She means to chase the square, grey van that has just passed the house. Izabella jumps on the bike, kicks away the stand and starts the machine with force. The two-stroke engine roars into life and there's a sudden smell of fuel. She's confident with the bike and ready to leave.

Marta is wide-eyed at her mother's actions, brow furrowed in confusion. Izabella knows Jolan, who rents a room next door, will take good care of her daughter and siblings while she is gone. Aunt Joli, as the children call her, is a good friend and they often sit outside together as the children play on the street. Izabella knew she would have to explain her actions in hushed tones later. Or maybe Joli would read between the lines and know better than to ask. It would be harder to explain to the children. The Soviet 'liberation' had not been anything like the people had imagined. Because no one could imagine this life for themselves.

I can't think about that now, Izabella thought to herself, I must focus on getting to my husband. She clenched her teeth and set off as fast as she could to pursue the van that had already reached the church and was heading south on the road to Szeged. The others can only stand and watch as she heads off, the dust of the road rising to obscure their view.

She hadn't thought to put on the trench coat she normally rode in, but she didn't feel the cold or worry about the chance of dirt on her clothes today as she sped past Balástya. The narrow road took her alongside the farms and fields, she knew well. As usual it was quiet and she saw only one horse and cart going about its business. She had a narrow miss with a motorcycle hurtling in the opposite direction, but Izabella kept the van in her sight, eyes fixed on the window at the back where she had seen her husband's hopeful face.

András had been gone for six months now. Taken in the February snow, the imprints from his boots the only evidence of a scuffle that ended in him being dragged away. Imprisoned without a trial for speaking out against the regime when he saw an opportunity to rouse the people into rebellion and restore democracy to the country and people he loved. Every morning she hoped she would receive word he was to be freed. Every evening she went to bed disappointed.

Was it easier for him, she wondered? It was not the first time András had been arrested and detained for his views. In 1947, he had been a leader of the Social Democratic Party and had worked to expose the Communist Party's plans for voting fraud, when they encouraged partisans to vote for them under more than one name. It was not a surprise when he was arrested for his political activities in 1949. But then it was official, and his sentence was set for four years. Izabella had been married to Lajos at the time, of course; they were busy rebuilding their life together after the war. When András was taken that first time, she would have been pregnant with Gyorgy. How things had changed. Now she was married again and a mother of three children. And his time, there was no trial, no paperwork, no trace, nothing.

She didn't think she could cope if his sentence lasted as long as the last one, life had taught her much could change in a year, let alone several. When András finally returned to his village in 1953 it was to find Izabella a widow, but if he was gone for that length of time again little Laszlo would barely remember him. And in 1949, his name and sentence had been recorded. Who knew if the authorities would admit to how many they had tortured, killed and imprisoned during the revolution and thereafter. The lucky ones had been exiled. Would they ever release András, or might he 'disappear' entirely?

One thing was certain; you couldn't trust the government and those that ran it. They had stormed through Budapest with ruthless cruelty. Overhead military planes opened fire on civilians young and old and tanks ploughed through anyone and anything that stood in their way. Rebels took over the radio stations and built barricades but it was not enough. With no help from the West, the people and their home-made grenades and Molotov cocktails were soon overpowered, and rebels were slaughtered en masse. Russian machine guns fired across the Danube, the city's beauty spots were turned to rubble, and 2,500 Hungarians died. In the face of the never-ending tyranny, two hundred thousand abandoned their homeland altogether. Twelve days of revolt in one autumn could not undo years of oppression.

Now the Kremlin was calling the shots and the authorities worried even less about being seen as decent. Several years ago, Laszlo had seen his father being beaten unconscious by the police. His body dragged to the village tap to revive him. Now, the leaders of the rebellion, like Imre Nagy, had been executed, the people that followed them paid in blood. János Kádár betrayed the revolution and in return for his loyalty to the Soviets was installed as a puppet leader. Where would the tyranny end?

Hungary had been so used to living under a dictatorship, the despot Mátyás Rákosi had led Hungary's communist party from 1945 to 1956, first as General Secretary of the Hungarian Communist Party and later holding the same post with the Hungarian Working People's Party. Loyal to Russia, Rákosi slowly but surely purged all his political rivals and their supporters, to become Prime Minister. Even he fell foul of his masters though, being forced to give up his position to Nagy. There had been some hope then, but that too had floundered. The revolution exposed the level of savagery that the authorities would use to ensure its will was met.

And perhaps even worse than András being taken (and before that her brother, Gyuri, too, she suspected) was the fact that she wasn't able to explain it to her children, to tell them what was really happening. Marta was at school now, being told day after day that communism was good for society, and that deviation from the Party was wrong. And the children would never hear a bad word against the Party from their parents because that would spell trouble for them, for everyone. No one was free to express an opinion in Hungary while the Soviets were in charge.

Marta loved celebrating her birthday on 1 May because of the national holiday and festivities. Her mother didn't have the heart to tell her daughter that the mass parades the communists arranged to celebrate what they had rebranded as the 'International Day of the Struggle and Celebration of the Workers for Peace and Socialism' were compulsory and not quite what they seemed.

There had always been a 'labour day' holiday, of course, where the workers could look forward to a day off, but the Party now insisted everyone troupe past guests of honour waving Party-approved banners and flags. There was no rest for the people of Hungary. No day off from their toil. Still Izabella tried to do the best she could to make sure Marta's day wasn't ruined, spending the morning baking, so that the day would be full of tasty treats. She made up for a shortfall in earnings by selling some of the items Aranka sent them from England. There was often coffee and chocolate, and always clothes from her stylish former sister-in-law.

She didn't even tell the children when András was bundled into a vehicle early one Sunday morning. She'd avoided the children's questions at the time, and now they no longer asked.

It wasn't unusual for people to disappear these days, and somehow, everyone knew not to discuss who was and wasn't here, and why. András had been so sure change was coming this time, that the West would come and support a system change and stop the suffering.

Would she ever see András again? Would she want to? The ones that came back were often changed. Banned from working, from meeting and talking to people and to groups, and even from going into restaurants and shops. They lived in fear of being reported and taken again. Everyone was afraid, afraid of saying the wrong thing to the wrong people, afraid of being identified as an enemy of the state, afraid of being caught without papers or caught listening to a foreign radio station. The police carried heavy batons and you avoided them, avoided looking at them.

You couldn't hold a decent job unless you were a Party member with your little red book. Anyone that had a council job, anyone that wanted to teach, they all had to toe the party line. There was no room for free thinking or independent views. For those willing to play the game, the rewards included a better pay scale and safety. While the schoolchildren sang about the glory of the Party, with their red neckerchiefs tied proudly, all Izabella saw was the corruption of communism. The people that the Party apparently loved so very much didn't even have meat for the table.

Some people kept up the fight, of course. There was the time the billboard outside the school declaring 'éljen a szovjet unió' (Long live the Soviet Union) was doctored. Just by adding an 'f' to the verb, the poster was changed to mean 'be afraid of the Soviet Union. That was both clever and funny! But within the day that was painted over. But it was a brave person that chose to openly oppose this barbaric government now. They probably didn't have a household of children to care for alone, Izabella thought.

Izabella knew she was getting closer to Szeged when she reached Lake Fehér. Since this was the only road running to the town, keeping the van in sight had not been a problem up until now. But the town was larger than her village and she was only familiar with certain parts of it. As she followed the van it turned into town and Izabella could see the twin spires of the Votive Church ahead of her. Soon they were crossing the Belvárosi Bridge over the Tisza, where more roads converged behind the park. Now it was getting more difficult to keep up with the van that held her husband and Izabella tried to increase her speed without being too visible. Suddenly a gaggle of students crossed the road in front of her and Izabella swerved to avoid them, checking behind her to make sure she'd not alarmed them too much.

When she returned her focus to the front she could no longer see the van. She scanned left and right, still nothing. 'No, no, no,' she thought to herself. She slowed her pace; travelling up and down any roads she came to, hoping the van was parked up, hoping she would see it again. But the roads began to look the same, and she wondered if she was repeating her search or simply heading further and further away from where she'd lost the vehicle. Finally, she pulled up alongside the pavement and her shoulders dropped. She felt tired. It was time to go home. Any trace of András was long gone.

Chapter 11

Izabella, 1952, Kistelek

So there it was, a thin piece of paper from the Land Registry Office that passed as a receipt for what she had just witnessed. The court order was double stamped and a reference number was inked in on the top right. This crumpled document marked the official 'transfer' of her home and shop into the hands of the state.

Hungarian citizens were no longer allowed to own buildings or businesses because that was apparently not in the interests of the state. Property-owning Hungarians such as the Seilers were holding the country back, according to those in power, who somehow seemed to have more of their fair share and yet were not questioned or penalised for it. After Auschwitz, after Bergen-Belsen, who would have thought that the Red Army saviour that had liberated their country all those years ago would become instead its new torturer? And an arguably worse one at that? Its methods all the worse for being carried out in piecemeal, slowly stripping away all that the people valued, until they were left barren and bare. And so often done in secret.

Izabella stared down at the useless document in her hands. Once again I have nothing, she thought. Just like that, in a matter of minutes, all that my family and the family of my husband have worked for is gone.

Lifting her head, she stared into the eyes of the policeman; the polished leather visor of his peaked cap mostly hiding his face. Did she know him? Was he someone from Kistelek village itself? Was he well rewarded for his loyalty to the state and where did he rest his head at night, she wondered? How many other lives had he destroyed today, how many mothers had he made homeless? What kind of countryman would willingly do this to another? Was he the same man that had jeered at the carts that took the Jews to the ghettos and camps? The policeman stared back impassively.

But perhaps she should consider herself lucky, she thought wryly. After all, she was actually being allowed to stay in the house that she formally owned and, she laughed, would be able to pay rent to the treasury for the privilege! She would even be able to continue to work in the 'government's' shop too, for a pittance, of course! It certainly was a one-way street this 'workers' state'.

She realised the policeman was still standing opposite her, waiting for a response. Was she supposed to say 'thank you' after she had handed over her keys to him? She was hardly going to argue about it was she? On top of his tunic with its shiny brass buttons running from top to bottom, he wore a Sam Browne belt, the narrower strap reaching diagonally over his right shoulder. On the central strap a pouch held spare cartridges for the gun he tucked tightly into his left side. The other man had a gun, too. Marching boots and breeches completed their uniforms; they were more like soldiers than policemen. This was a garb the ordinary people had come to hate; a representation of a police state that was in service to its totalitarian emancipator.

The force had a list you see, and day by day they worked through this written reckoning. They went from house to house and shop to shop in the village, claiming everything for the state. Taking the jobs and livelihoods of everyday people, young and old, turning families into the street and ruining lives and futures for generations. The premise was that if you owned land you were a class enemy, a hangover from the days of the Magyar somehow. Your hard work meant nothing. Anyone that owned property had an unfair advantage and everyone should be on a level playing field. Except, of course, if you carried out the orders for the state. Everyone was equal, although some were just more equal. Particularly those that knew people in the 'right' office.

The local farmers had already suffered this indignation, of course, having had their land taken away and their production quotas set by outsiders that knew nothing of the ways of the countryside, forced to turn over what they produced to collectives, and go hungry because of it. The authorities didn't like the thought of swathes of economically independent people living in the countryside and made their lives as hard as they could. To avoid this constant victimisation, some had moved to the cities to start a new life. It was a life they didn't understand and weren't qualified for, but they hoped they would come to prefer it to being left to work their fields and animals for so little reward. Many were disappointed, of course. Private business owners met the same fate, too. One member of the

Seiler family had owned the petrol station and adjacent house. Now he still worked and lived there but the profits were no longer his to enjoy. Put simply, it was demoralising. How could you care enough to get up each day, and open the business shutters, when this is what you faced?

Nationalisation, industrialisation and indoctrination were the favoured government policies. It was no coincidence that those that spoke out against the regime were also the ones more likely to lose the right to even live in their newly repossessed homes. If they were actually seen again that is, because so many outspoken people had this 'habit' of vanishing. The Soviets learnt a trick or two from the Nazis, and thousands of real and supposed enemies had been interned in camps not too dissimilar to the concentration camps. Sometimes whole families were sent away to places like Recsk, Kistarcsa, Tiszalök and Kazincbarcika, each surrounded by barbed wire. Enemies were silenced by any means necessary, regardless of whether your politics were far right like the Nazis, or far left like the Soviets. These extremists had more in common with each other than they realised.

Those that held religious views were also disproportionately penalised because religion was considered an enemy of the state, too. Imagine there being any higher order than the government? There was nothing worse than citizens that felt they had a moral obligation to their god over what the state told them to do. Obedience to the authorities wasn't optional. Church-owned schools were shut down and students from religious backgrounds were discriminated against when applying for college and university. Religious leaders were edged out by fair means or foul, a false accusation here and an enforced emigration there. Party stooges were fed into the churches and the State Church Bureau took charge of it all.

And as for us Jews? Imagine you had been lucky enough to survive terrors such as the Nazi death or labour camps, and had returned home and quietly worked hard to rebuild your life as best you could. Keeping your head down, not dwelling on who had betrayed you, willing yourself a future. Turns out, putting the past behind you wasn't enough. You were going to suffer again under communism. Jews were not welcome in the world vision that Stalin held either. It had happened in the Czechoslovak Republic just last year. Fourteen members of the Communist party there were arrested and charged with being Titoists and Zionists. Eleven were hanged, three received life sentences instead. It was a stark reminder there could be no other heroes to heed than Stalin and his henchmen, no god higher than their own earthly leaders. To Izabella this great 'Union' to fight the West didn't sound all that different to Hitler's great plan to create the perfect world dominated by his 'superior' race.

And there was no recourse for those unfairly treated. The law courts were not as they had been. More than a thousand judges had been dismissed after the war, with all the new faces that replaced them loyal to the Party instead. Now your status could easily be held against you, so the bourgeois and aristocrats and even the peasant kulaks, always came off worse. The 'confessions' the accused proffered might owe more to the conditions they were given under than any resemblance to the truth. Executions for political reasons were common. And family members and loved ones of the accused weren't safe either. Would this uncertainty, this suffering, always characterise her life, Izabella wondered?

And so it was on this clear April morning, Izabella had heard a tremendous thumping on the front door, answering to find two state policemen there. They had marched in with a labourer, who immediately set to work bricking up the doorway between the middle room and the shop. They didn't speak much, and didn't need to, Izabella knew why they were there and that she couldn't stop them. She watched in disbelief as brick after brick was slammed down, the metallic scraping of the trowel setting her teeth on edge as it scraped a layer of mortar in between each of the red rectangles. And, of course, they left a mess behind with their shoddy workmanship. It wasn't just dollops of cement that lay in the dust at her feet now.

As if her life was not desperate enough, Lajos was surely dying in hospital and she struggled to run the home and shop alongside being a mother of two as it was. Now that the state owned the shop, they could choose someone in favour to run it too, and then she would have no job either because she had been branded 'bourgeois'. Oh yes, she was sure that those in the local Communist party would fare well when the spoils were 'redistributed'. Izabella knew it would be Party members that were able to live in the grandest houses paying low rent and decide exactly where they'd like to work for a high salary. Owning a 'little red book' was the key to prosperity now.

And she also knew that after her house, the policemen would visit the Kiss family next door. The rent they paid Lajos and her for both their home and pharmacy, would now go to the state too, reducing her income even more. How would she manage, how would they eat, where would she work? Would her troubles and days of hunger never end? Thank goodness she now found the people of Kistelek kind, and that they always addressed her respectfully. Perhaps it was because the Seilers were hard workers and fair traders, or perhaps it was because all the people were now united in their hatred of the Hungarian Communist Party, even if they could not speak of it openly. And she had some savings after all. She would do the best she could with what she had. She was no stranger to adversity, and she knew that one thing for sure, she was a survivor.

She thought of poor Marta, who would have to sleep in this room each night, the bricked up door a permanent reminder of the life they had led as shopkeepers. Marta loved the comings and goings of the shop, the people, the goods they sold. She took an interest in everything and remained untroubled by the politics of the world around her. Perhaps she could move a piece of furniture to block the unsightly bricks that were now where the door had been.

It was clear to Izabella she would have to shield the children from the worst of their new situation, just like she had not told them how seriously ill their father was. The children mustn't know about the worry of putting food on the table. They mustn't realise that life no longer offered any security. And that anything and everything you valued could be taken away without warning. It was her job as their mother to protect them from these harsh realities of life as long as she could.

She hoped one day her children might find a way to leave Hungary altogether and be able to live in a freer society. A society where you were judged fairly and not on how you looked, which building your parents worshipped in or what political beliefs you held. A country where you could work hard and reap the benefits of those efforts. A place where you would not go hungry or be scared for the future. It wasn't such a big ask was it? She thought.

But enough of these far-fetched dreams, she told herself. Right now, thought Izabella, I must work out what I will do next.

Chapter 12

Marta, 2000, Manchester

Marta picked up the faded cardboard folder she had left on the small wooden table to the right of the sofa and removed the tired elastic bands that had held it together all this time. Last night she had been overwhelmed with what she had read and had put the documents aside in order to go to sleep but now, refreshed from the night's rest, she was eager to learn more about the secrets and significance these largely unnoticed papers had held tight for so many years.

Some of the letters were handwritten, some typed, others in pencil that had lost so much of the definition they were virtually impossible to read. The letters were sent by her grandmother, her father and even by her mother, Izabella. Some of the letters were written in Hungarian, others in German. Translating from Hungarian was a laborious task, first making the literal conversion and then rewriting the words so that they made sense in English. She couldn't read those written in German.

Stored with the letters were various photographs that Marta recognised as ones that had been displayed at her aunt's house for many years.

She turned again to the words that had stayed in her mind since she first read them. Her father's words: 'My grief is like emptying an ocean with a spoon.'

He was writing to his sister, Marta's Aunt Aranka, with whom she had lived when she first moved to England, about the loss of their mother. His letter is dated 6 January 1946. Marta had now learned that by this time he had returned to Kistelek after being freed by the Soviets from the labour camp he had once again been called to in February the previous year. He knew that his mother had been deported along with the other Jewish women, children and remaining men in the village and that from Kistelek they were taken to Szeged, where they stayed for several days. After this mutual connections had told him that his mother was then sent to Auschwitz on a 'hospital' wagon with any other sick prisoners. He discovered the wagons were packed with eighty people at a time, but that two sisters had gently tended to his mother, as if she were their own. But he also had to tell his sister that, like everyone else in that wagon, their mother never returned to their homes at the end of the war. He explained that their mother's ill health made it more likely that she died en route to the infamous death camp rather than terrified for her life in a gas chamber. Small mercies, Marta had thought when she had read that.

In his letters Lajos describes to Aranka the physical conditions he finds himself living in after the war as well as how he feels about his life. While he has a house to live in, their home and business have been looted and he explains that 'not even a single handkerchief' has been left. He also details his time in Budapest after his initial release when he was suffering from typhus and pneumonia. He relays how he lay unconscious in hospital for two weeks and that he believes his survival is miraculous. He also tells of how, unaware of the repercussions it would bring, that upon finding he was free, and after months of starvation, he had eaten without restraint. But this instinct to suddenly feast had caused a perforated stomach serious enough that had required Lajos to have an operation.

Marta can only guess how horrific this all had been for Aranka to read, so far away in England, powerless to help. It would not have made it any easier for her when at the same time that, as Marta can see from the collected letters, Aranka was also receiving letters from family members telling them of their concerns for Lajos, who they said was sleeping under just a rug. Perhaps this explains why Aranka continued to help her mother long after Lajos's death, regularly sending packages to help the family. And also why Marta found herself living in London all those years ago. The letters added another perspective to everything that Marta thought she knew. How strange to realise all these things had affected her life, and yet she had remained unaware of them.

The letter vocalising her father's grief had been just one of a cache of papers that traced the family news as it travelled back and forth across the miles, the borders and the seas that separated them. Marta was shocked when she read the words and, as she translated from Hungarian, she had found she was crying. Her father expressed his grief so poetically her heart ached for his loss. She knew so little about her father and his family, and possessed only one photograph of him herself. Her mother had rarely spoken of him as she had grown up, although she remembers visiting his grave regularly. Apart from this she has just one treasured memory of her father from her early childhood. It is of pretending to use his motorbike, with him holding her on the seat as if she were an accomplished rider. Now Marta was learning more about him and his life, and not all that she was learning was easy to accept.

Through reading his words, Marta felt a connection to the father she barely remembered click into place. Knowing how he had felt about the hardships he had faced somehow made him seem far more real than ever before, and she could almost touch the emotion he described. At its first reading, it had been so upsetting to understand the story of what had happened to him and her grandmother that she could not return to his letters for hours. When she did she discovered family trauma, grief and emotions, trapped in time, written on pages so thin it felt as if they could evaporate before her eyes. The fragile nature of the letters brought with them a sense of urgency.

Marta found it hard to believe that so much of the past had been waiting patiently here in this folder for her to pore over. With snippets of news here and there she began fitting the pieces of information together to give her a clear picture, as if it were a puzzle that she had long since lost the cover image of as it had been passed down the generations. When she first received the folder she had been a busy woman, combining motherhood with running a business. Now, all these years later, with her own family grown and safely flown the nest, finally she had found the time to sit down and examine the textures and tones of these individual leaves of her Hungarian family tree.

She traced the writing on the postcard she held from her grandmother, Cecilia, next. She now knew that this had been her final communication with her father, who was Cecilia's only son.

'They are taking us away tomorrow,' she wrote, her looped cursive hand naturally bolder in some areas as the ink flowed from her pen. Wide spaces between the words on this card contrasted sharply to her earlier letters, perhaps showing that she was in a hurry when she wrote it, or a sign that her health had deteriorated greatly. At the end of the card Cecilia added:

'Pray that I can see you again.

Many kisses
Your distraught mother'.

The message was written on an official, pre-stamped postcard and was addressed to Lajos Seiler in another part of Hungary. Sent on Saturday, 17 June in 1944 and barely legible, it had been confusing to read at first because it was not obvious to Marta why her father was not in his village alongside his mother, working in their businesses, as she had expected him to be.

But what Marta did quickly understand was that this dashed off note was the very last letter her grandmother had sent before being rounded up alongside the other Jews left in Kistelek to be taken to Auschwitz. It was the very last chance she had to speak to her son and would become her last mark on the world, documenting forever how she was treated in her final days. This hard-working matriarchal businesswoman and pillar of the Jewish community had been separated from her closest ally as she headed off to her death. Had Marta's grandmother understood what lay ahead? Marta felt her brow furrow as she imagined how desperate her grandmother must have felt as she wrote that message. It was her final goodbye to Lajos, and to the world.

Marta also felt a stab of guilt as she read her grandmother's words. It was a Jewish tradition to name a child after a dead relative you wished to remember, and never a living one. Marta had been given two first names, and the second one was that of her grandmother. Clearly her father had wanted to honour the mother he missed so very much when Marta was born. And yet she had always disliked the name, and feeling no connection to her namesake, Marta had long since cast it off not understanding its significance. Now she realised she wanted to learn more about this woman she was named after, a woman that had died amidst the chaos and brutality of the Holocaust. An event she hadn't fully understood until she decided to learn more about her faith as an adult.

In other letters her grandmother wrote of her declining health and how her life was changing. She spoke of how her carer was made to leave her house in tears by the authorities, now that Jews were no longer allowed staff. She gave the girl food and all that she could spare; aware the girl was now homeless. She also describes how she was frightened when she was reported for allowing a chink of light to be seen at her window after 9pm and that she expects to have the son of a German Supervisor billeted on the house soon, because as a Jew she was not allowed to live alone in a house with more than a certain number of rooms. She details the items the police have already confiscated from their home, and says how she has given many items away to neighbours for safe keeping. She shares her joy at receiving her son's letters and tells him she hopes that they will meet again soon, promising to send her son the necessities he needs, but lacks, at his work camp. Reading the letters over and over, and scouring the words for more clues about her family, Marta also feels that her grandmother gives her son some subtle hints about where she has hidden certain valuables.

In later letters, it's clear to Marta that her grandmother realises that as the war progresses her words are being read, and that she must not complain too much. Marta notices how Cecilia mentions her feelings of sadness and fear far less in the later letters as her grandmother instead peppers them with information about their friends and family; an illness here, a death there. The stories include those about a woman that refused to wear the yellow star and was apprehended, and another that was told she must leave her home. Marta can see her grandmother is aware all remaining Jews will be taken from their homes in the village at some point, although she is perhaps naively optimistic that a move to a shared house may mean she will have someone to care for her in her ill health. The concept of accommodation within a very basic and crowded ghetto is beyond Cecilia's imagination, of course.

Later Cecilia's letters detail the conditions in that ghetto, where Marta's grandmother found herself squashed into an attic room with thirty other women and too far away from the inadequate toilet. Marta smiles as she learns her grandmother was pleased to see her status in the community was upheld when she was chosen to share a mattress with the wife of a Rabbi. How funny, and yet how human, that this remains important to her in this dreadful situation when she is so poorly, thinks Marta. She wonders if her father smiled as he had read this too, all those years before her. A response shared across the generations and even time itself.

Cecilia mentions that the censorship of any messages they send has increased and says her health is worsening but, Marta notices, her grandmother is still looking for the good in the situation, as she explains how the ghetto is zealously cleaned by those that find themselves there. These small remarks help Marta build a picture of her grandmother's personality, what was important to her and how she reacted to her frightening change in circumstances.

Marta looks at the many letters. As Aranka's only living relative, she had inherited this bundle of documents when her aunt died in 1993. Unknowingly, she'd put them aside to be sorted through at a later date. But now, decluttering before she moved south to be closer to her daughters, Marta realised she had stumbled onto the most precious legacy her aunt could have left her. These letters held the story of how her family had experienced life in Hungary since the 1940s. She was the guardian of this account of her family's experience of both the Second World War and Soviet rule.

The letters showed how they had been treated as Jews and as business owners both under the Nazi-influenced Hungarian government, and then later by the Soviets she had regarded as their liberators and was taught to admire during her state education. They revealed a whole wealth of information that Marta had somehow not been told. So much so, it reminded her of the time she learnt of her father's death only through a playground taunt, rather than at the time it actually happened. It seemed she had lived in a protective bubble. A bubble she must now be brave enough to pop.

The letters made Marta consider how much her mother bore in silence and how that had impacted her relationship with her children. Marta now felt that Izabella had been so persecuted for so long that when Marta was young, her mother was simply 'going through the motions' of existing rather than truly living her life. In turn this explained how the family had moved to Budapest once Marta was living safely in England without it ever being discussed. At the time Marta thought it odd she had never been told of the plans, but now she understood that life had taught Izabella to live day by day and not look into the future. Izabella knew better than to take for granted the idea that you could do as you wanted.

Marta could see that her mother had worked her way through endless days of existence, getting up each and every day to face so much, then simply going to bed at the end of the day, knowing the next day would bring the same. And yet Marta had experienced a happy childhood, kept in blissful ignorance of her mother's struggles. As an adult she could see Izabella had worked hard to protect her daughter from the stark realities of hunger, insecurity and oppression. Her mother had been let down by the state time and time again, each political mood swing dealing her a poorer hand. She now realised how lucky she was to be sent off to England and Aunt

Aranka. It had changed the course of her life. Facilitating this new life for Marta had meant the world to Izabella.

Her grandmother's letters to her father, Lajos, were always handwritten, first in ink, and then later in pencil from the ghetto when pens became luxuries they did not have. The writing slanted to the left, her pressure on the pen variable. The dots on her 'i's were high and slightly to the right. She drew wide 'e' loops but her penmanship was narrow on the looped letters that rose or fell above the line. Her 't's were always crossed in the middle. There was hardly any white space left on the page with each of the lines tucked closely together as she tried to fit as many words as she could on the pages that she sent to her beloved son. Every inch of the letter was as precious to the sender as it was to the recipient.

At the very beginning, the letters from her father were written in his barely legible writing. But later, after he had settled more into his life again, he bought a typewriter frugally typing on both sides of the thin yellowy-brown paper. The impact of the keys on one side made it hard to see the words on the other side. Punctuation marks such as full stops and commas were typed with extra force, too, and time had made them stand out clearly across the page. Reading the letters, Marta discovered that his first typewriter had been one of his most prized possessions and that it was taken along with the other family valuables when anti-Semitic laws came into force from 1938 onwards and Jews were victimised and made to feel unwelcome. It was one of the items her father particularly minded being taken, and so she guessed it must have given him great satisfaction to buy another.

Marta was so glad that she had had the sense to examine the documents closely. They could easily have been tossed aside as she ruthlessly cleared out her belongings; there was already a large plastic rubbish sack of things she had decided to get rid of. It was fortunate that she was aware that in the next eighteen months or so, she'd be required to have pertinent documents ready to hand as she relocated and arranged her finances for a move. The papers had had a lucky escape. She must make sure that didn't happen again.

Marta had always felt that as long as people remembered you, you were still alive and felt ashamed that so many of her family were not spoken about regularly nor celebrated. She knew it was her job now to ensure that the memories her family had put down on paper were kept alive. But how? Perhaps her brother in Israel would want them she thought, or maybe Yad Vashem would keep them with its records.

These were avenues to explore another day, she told herself.

As a first step, today Marta decided she would sort out the letters and photographs properly. She planned to put them in some sort of order and then work out what she would do next. To ensure they were kept safe she had already written clearly across the front of the folder 'NEVER THROW AWAY', just in case the worst happened and her daughters, unaware of the significance of what was inside, and unable to read the foreign hand in which they were penned, threw them out.

Marta was clear of one thing, now these letters had come to light, they were too important to remain packed away. She knew it was her responsibility to bring these letters to the world. She owed it to her family, to her parents, to her aunt and perhaps mostly to her grandmother, the author of so many of the letters, to show how they had suffered and struggled – and also how they had strived and survived such cruelty, hardship and victimisation.

Taking her lead from *Tahara*, the selfless Jewish ritual of washing the dead, she would ensure the family history held within these letters was told and thereby give back to her family.

And while these documents told the story of her family, they could also come to teach the world about how to treat your fellow man.

Chapter 13

Lajos, 1935, Kistelek

Lajos placed the painted wooden sign he had made in the low square window to the right of the front door. He wanted as many people to see it as possible. He was pretty sure the village would soon be talking about this new service and his new skill.

It hadn't been too long ago that he'd taken the trip to Szeged to buy what he needed. He'd been fascinated to learn about this new technology, having read up on the developments in engineering since learning that news and sport reports were being broadcast in places like America and Argentina. Now that thermionic valves had been developed it had revolutionised radio receivers and transmitters. And he was Kistelek's first ever radio repairman.

His plan had been simple enough. He had purchased a radio set from the city, and returned home. Once back at his kitchen table, he laid out some newspaper, placed the radio upon it and carefully took it apart. He noted where each of the components lay and how they fitted together. And then, piece by careful piece, he put the radio back together and made sure it worked again. He did this several times until he could reassemble the radio in a matter of minutes.

In this way he learnt what was underneath the glossy wooden casing and how each part played its own role. He noticed how the condenser secured to the baseboard, screwing vertically in place and examined the delicately thin wire of the coupling transformer. There was also a wavechange switch and a dial marked with wavelengths to be considered and investigated. Each component was bare mounted and Lajos had to ever-so-carefully remove and retain each of the screws that held the chassis together so that the radio would look as good as new once complete.

It gave Lajos great satisfaction to hang the 'Radios Repaired' sign. The cream letters were painted neatly onto a black background, and a double border drew attention to the proud declaration. He was technically minded and liked to be first to appreciate a novel invention. His home boasted the first 'English' toilet and the one and only hot water bath in the village. He considered himself ahead of his time, and aware of developments across the world. He spoke not just his native Hungarian but also German and English. Just because he was from a small Hungarian village, it didn't mean he wasn't worldly wise.

He also got a buzz out of understanding new technology. And wow, what a technology radio was, thought Lajos, starting out as early as the 1880s with the discovery of radio waves. An Italian chap called Marconi had taken it from there, applying the science to produce radio communications for the military and marines. Inventors all over the world worked on new developments; over in India, Bose used millimetre-range-wavelength microwaves, while other demonstrations took place in English universities. Marconi opened an actual radio factory in England in 1912 to produce many sets at a time. That scientists were working together on this development in countries both near and far intrigued Lajos. The idea that people could and would be connected by radio all over the world was astonishing. However, Lajos also knew there was often nothing more satisfying than sending a neatly typed letter off to a loved one, full of news and love.

Back at home in 1925, Lajos was excited to learn that the Tungsram company was now making radio sets too and not long after that Philips and Orion also released models onto the Hungarian market. While originally many radio sets had been functional boxes, some of the sets he'd seen were breathtakingly beautiful wooden boxes with stylish decoration, just like a small piece of modern furniture! With arched tops and decorative grilles to cover the speakers, they reminded Lajos of tiny cathedrals built to worship technology! He could almost imagine the boxes housing tiny people rushing backwards and forwards to wrangle the components into working.

And just before Christmas that year, Hungary had launched its own national radio station, Budapest 1, broadcast from Csepel. Lajos had listened in with a relative that lived in the city and heard the very first words: 'Hallo–hallo! Here's the transmitter of the Hungarian radio broadcasting with 2 kW on 565 metres AM.' Of course, not everyone could tune in until national broadcasting started three years later, when the Csepel transmitter was replaced with what Lajos knew was the 20 kW-strong Lakihegy Tower. He watched with interest as two new towers were built in 1932 and 1933, by which time he heard there were three hundred thousand radio listeners. What a world we live in, he had thought to himself.

Of course, an interest in engineering wasn't the only thing motivating Lajos to offer a repair service for this new technology. He also saw a business opportunity and took it. He was certain he had enterprise in his blood, like so many of his Jewish brothers. Why you only had to look at his ancestors to see they knew how to get a business up and running successfully.

First Seiler in Kistelek had arrived in 1860, and by 1882 most of the shops in the village were owned by Jews. That first arrival, and several of his sons, ran a butcher's shop. Perhaps surprisingly, the shop supplied pork to the famous salami factory, but since it was only actually eating pork that was forbidden by their religion, raising and selling it was fine. Other branches of the family went on to run a flour store, a building society/bank and a friendly food and drink venue open to both men and women known as a *kaszino*. Yet another cousin ran the petrol station at the edge of the village, where all the vehicles going in and out would stop for fuel. Still more enterprising, he thought, were the owners of a food shop that came up with idea to lend out all the crockery you needed for a celebratory event, as long as you bought your supplies from them. The local Jewish community even ran their own private school for decades until free schooling was provided for all in the 1900s. Yes, we Seilers and we Jews are a resourceful bunch, he mused.

As for him, well he shared this paint shop with his dear mother, Cecilia Lowy. She was a widow twice over, his father, Imre Seiler, had died when Lajos was just 2 and his sister Aranka was aged 5. Lajos's baby sister, Irma, was born in the same year their father died but lived for just two short years. Lajos barely remembered baby Irma, or his father, but counted himself lucky as he had lots of happy family memories of his stepfather, Mikso Lowy, who stepped into the paternal role and proved to be a loving parent to him and Aranka. Unfortunately, like many Jewish men, Mikso had fought and died for Hungary in the First World War, and now his name was one of the six etched on the village war memorial. Five of those men were from Jewish families.

Cecilia's life seemed so full of tragedy, losing not one but two husbands. Lajos had nothing but admiration for how his mother had coped with all these hardships. She ran the paint shop and other business concerns, including rental properties, on her own for years. She worked hard and was an astute businesswoman. Little surprise then that she was on the all-important Ladies Guild, and also one of the town's decision-makers. In Kistelek there were fifty-seven people that were allowed to make decisions on behalf of the village. They earned the right to be part of this esteemed group of local representatives because they paid the most tax. They were the success stories of the village if you like – and they and their opinions – were respected as such. The fact that they were all Jewish, bar one, was irrelevant because being Jewish then was not considered significant.

When it was time for Aranka to find a husband, the local male Jewish population was small and proved to be mostly relations of some kind. Accordingly, Lajos's mother had looked further afield for a good match. In the end, Aranka married Izso Weiss, a timber merchant from Vienna, in a very grand ceremony indeed. At the wedding the groom sported a silk top hat, and the couple rode a magnificent horse carriage covered in white flowers. Aranka now lived a very comfortable life in Austria and Cecilia did not need to worry about her wellbeing. What Jewish mother could ask for more! Aranka's marriage and subsequent move left Lajos and his mother to run the businesses together in Kistelek. They made a great team, and neither of them worried about seeking out their own future spouse.

The other aspect of radio technology that Lajos greatly admired was that it allowed him to listen in on political developments. Hungary had seen so much upheaval since the end of the Great War. The changes often worried Lajos, who knew how they could affect his family's safety and livelihood.

In 1919 the communists established the Hungarian Soviet Republic, which lasted just four months. But it was long enough for the 'Red Terror' to scar the country, brutal government suppression targeting anti-communist forces. A backlash was inevitable and between 1919 and 1921, the 'White Terror' began, with communists, industrial workers and Jews now the persecuted. Thousands were imprisoned without trial and hundreds killed. The violence was carried out by counter-revolutionary soldiers and targeted anyone that was thought to be supportive of Hungary's short-lived Soviet republic.

When the Treaty of Trianon was signed in 1920, Hungary lost much of its land and population. The bordering countries like Romania, Czechoslovakia and the Kingdom of Serbs, Croats and Slovenes gained the land and people. Hungary's economic assets like timber, iron ore and arable land now belonged to these other nations and so Hungary had to become a trading nation to survive. Now Jews were just one of the minorities, making up only a few per cent of the overall population.

The new Prime Minister, István Bethlen, took office in 1921 when the country was virtually penniless, and Lajos listened to the speeches he gave promising to strengthen the economy. Bethlen borrowed 50 million US dollars from the League of Nations, and forged positive relationships with the British, the US and Italy. The news seemed to show things were picking up, with national income climbing by 20 per cent, yet Hungarian peasants were still living hand to mouth, and the working class and those in rural areas still struggled.

Lajos had listened in horror as the Wall Street crash in 1929 was announced; the world slipped into the Great Depression and grain prices plummeted. Of course, he knew Hungary would suffer, and so it was inevitable that people would lose jobs and their incomes, with the country plunging into poverty yet again. Then the news reported that Bethlen had resigned, and Gyula Károlyi was appointed in his place. The news didn't get any better that year and then in 1932 it was the turn of Gyula Gömbös to take the premiership. Lajos had his reservations about this man; although his party included Jewish members, this was a right-wing leader that had an anti-Semitic past and embraced Mussolini, and had even met with Hitler.

With this swing to the right, Lajos had begun to feel uncomfortable with the way Hungary was developing. For him his radio was a lifeline, helping him keep on top of the news so that he could plan in advance and protect himself and his family. That's why he liked to tune his radio into overseas stations, just to get another point of view to what was broadcast nationally.

Listening to the radio always helped Lajos stay one step ahead of what was to come. Which was to become more and more important.

Chapter 14

Izabella, 1948, Kistelek

As Izabella stirred the steaming pot, the familiar scent of the paprika-spiced meat met her nose, and she knew the dish would soon be ready. Her husband said there was nothing quite like her home-cooked *gulyás*, especially when it was served alongside the *tarhonya* made in their own back yard. Dear Lajos, their life together was going so well. Together, out of the wreckage of their lives, they had built this their home and their successful business, too. And they had their little Marta, her hair as poker straight as Izabella's, but not anywhere near her jet black locks in colour. Next year, there would be another baby also. Would it be a boy or a girl, Izabella wondered?

Yes, Izabella thought to herself, as she added a final pinch of seasoning, I should be free from worry at last.

And yet, Izabella knew she could never really be happy. Life had taught her to expect the worst and she found it was hard to settle even when all was well. Would it last? She always asked.

This nagging dissatisfaction that plagued her even now was also due in part to the fact that Gyorgy was not here to share her joy at this new life. And as long as her dear older brother was missing, she would feel as if a shadow was cast across a part of her heart. Where was he? And was he okay? She asked herself these questions again and again, day after day, sometimes even every hour, as she struggled to put Gyorgy out of her mind.

When she had made her way back to Kistelek after her time in Belsen, Izabella had one clear intention, and that was to find her parents and her siblings. She wanted to see if they had survived the war and what was left for them together as a family. Like many Jews after the war, she had other options; she could have built a new life where she was or she could have moved abroad to start over, many had left for Israel, for example. But Izabella chose home, Kistelek.

By some miracle, she had been reunited with them all except perhaps the one she loved the most. She knew that many, many Jewish families had not been so lucky to have most of the family survive. Some, like her, had been widowed, some had lost their children and, perhaps most heart wrenchingly of all, some had been made orphans by the war and were left unclaimed in hospitals and centres for the displaced. In fact, some people said that only a third of Hungarian Jews had lived.

Indeed, she knew many in the village less fortunate than her, not least her own Lajos, who had lost his mother. Everyone had lost someone. Lorant's two boys did not return for a start, Maca's family lost Gyuri, Bela Seiler's family was missing Teri and both Laci P and Tusi's husbands were not back. Only Eta from the Schreger family survived, while all the Piroska family were gone. An entire family erased. Perhaps then, Izabella thought, she should be grateful to be alive and to be reunited with most of her closest family?

But Izabella didn't feel grateful or lucky.

The last time she had seem Gyorgy was a year before the war had ended. He had left, as he had done many times before, when called up to work for the army. Because he was a Jew, he wasn't trusted to serve in any other way than with his labour. Accordingly, he no longer wore a uniform and his 'weapon' was merely a shovel. He was often gone for four or five months at a time, but he had always returned safely. True he had been exhausted and hungry then, but he was home, for a while at least.

Later she had learnt about the true horror of conditions at these work camps from Lajos, who suffered the same fate. Unfortunately, the two men had not been sent to the same place as workers were simply called up in birth date order and dispersed randomly as needed at the time. This was how family and friends lost touch, but also how sometimes news of a loved one came through when a man noticed another face from his village or community.

When at camp, there was the bad weather, inadequate clothing, lack of food and epidemics of typhus and dysentery to survive. This was on top of regular beatings and humiliations at the hands of many of the camp guards. Izabella was horrified to hear that the working days could last an agonising fourteen hours, wondering how Gyorgy had coped with such hardship and pressure. Lajos told her that the Jewish labourers were treated brutally by Hungarian soldiers, and then the Germans arrived. The Nazis quickly took over the running of the camps with the work and conditions the same, although there was a notable added sense of urgency and danger.

Towards the end of the war when the Russians were advancing, Lajos had told his wife that many of the detainees were marched hundreds of miles to the border with Austria to dig fortifications. He said that many, of course, died en route, pushed to the edge of what a human body could bear. He described how corpses, hastily dug graves and ownerless belongings littered the route. Izabella had seen these ghostly trails herself, framed by the train window as she travelled back from Belsen to Kistelek. In fact, it seemed to Izabella a miracle that any did live to tell of their treatment after enduring so much. And those that survived the marches, as she herself had done as she was herded from Auschwitz to Bergen-Belsen, told of how once they arrived at their new destinations they worked on and on still, in the bitter cold, without the proper equipment and without sleep.

Izabella knew that Lajos had been lucky in some ways, too. When the Red Army breached the border, they took the Germans in charge of his camp prisoner but allowed the labourers to flee; tired, skinny little men dressed in rags, running for their lives if they still could. She knew some had made it home to tell of their experience, but also that some died of exhaustion or the after effects of typhus on what they had hoped was their journey to freedom. What a cruel trick life has played on those poor souls. They had been set free, simply to die. Perhaps some were only a few miles from home and reuniting with their loved ones when their bodies just couldn't take any more.

Of course, those that came back brought solid news of those that had died and so those that loved them could grieve. But many, like Gyorgy, remained unaccounted for. There was no news, no trace. Did they die in a camp, on a march or clearing minefields, their families were left to wonder? Were they cold, alone and frightened as they passed? Did anyone comfort them in those final hours of life? Or perhaps they were still alive but lost, in hospital unable to talk or remember, or unable to get home for another reason? This not knowing, the speculation, was an endless torment for their loved ones that could do little more than wait.

In an attempt to calm the post-war chaos, the military were trying to restrict people moving about now, too, meaning that these lost relatives might be stuck somewhere and desperately needing help to come home. The helplessness now tormented so many wives and so many mothers. And sisters like Izabella, too.

Then, little by little, the villagers began to hear hushed talk that many of those in work camps were simply considered by the Soviet soldiers to be part of the Hungarian Army, and that they had been kept as prisoners of war. Now these poor souls stood as captives alongside their former captors and their endless days of work continued. Treated as if they were the same as their former guards. These poor people, barely alive from months and maybe even years of forced labour, were still slaves, just with a new keener and victorious master. And ironically working alongside those that had formerly tormented them.

The problem was that while the war had ended, the battlefield of Hungary lay in ruins. And the Soviets had big plans for these lands it now occupied as the spoils of that war.

But to put those plans into action it needed a large workforce. The authorities found that workforce in the towns and villages they had invaded under the guise of liberation. The Red Army began to round up more people for their work camps rather than look to release those it found already incarcerated in camps. Sometimes these quarries were marched to a bigger city to be put to work, other times people were loaded into cattle wagons; many Hungarians were taken to other countries like Romania and Moldova to work, and some were sent as far away as the desolate and inhospitable Siberia. Izabella thought it was state-sponsored kidnap and that perhaps her brother was one of the victims of this crime. For many, it seemed the truth about 'liberation' was that while the burden the Nazis had brought was gone the people were simply labouring under another yoke.

And as time wore on Izabella heard that the authorities were now taking anyone that spoke up against them to these camps too, now known by the Russian acronym 'Gulag'. It killed two birds with one stone, ridding the villages of someone that might encourage the people to speak up and rebel, and also adding to the workforce that was so desperately needed. And it was a deterrent. If you wanted to stay safe, you stayed silent.

Izabella despaired; how would she find Gyorgy if he was in one of these camps and the camps were being built up rather than closed down? Everyone knew it was impossible to try and escape if you had been taken to the cold and barren parts of Russia. Without food and decent clothes you couldn't make it out alive even if the guards didn't shoot you as you ran. And she knew she couldn't ask anyone official about where her brother might be now without risking her own internment, because the Gulags weren't to be spoken of out loud. No, honesty was not the best policy if she wanted to remain safely with her husband and daughter.

Instead, she listened constantly to the mass radio broadcasts that listed who had been found, and who was being looked for. She also approached the organisations that were trying to trace the missing and displaced. But, like the many other desperate relatives she found herself among, she discovered that rather than an ordered record, there was no one central authority in place and that the different groups were not linked up. The Red Cross, the Central Tracing Bureau and the Jewish Relief Unit were all working as hard as they could but the process was far from perfect. And it was not enough; Gyorgy was still not home.

The people running the searches were kind and understanding, they explained to Izabella that sometimes the Germans and their allies had destroyed documents from the camps they ran, and other times the records were incomplete. They also said that lists of those that shared family and common names couldn't distinguish between individuals, and that some people routinely used false names or details to avoid being identified as a Jew. The fact that a simple spelling mistake could mean a name was overlooked shocked Izabella. It filled her with hope that Gyorgy could still be alive and just unaccounted for, but it also terrified her, as she didn't know how they could be reunited amid all this bureaucratic confusion.

Learning more about the process, Izabella was told that even graves were checked to see how many bodies they held, and that the route of death marches were retraced in the search for missing camp inmates. Those that witnessed the marches were interviewed, too, and asked who and what they remembered. They didn't always remember much, of course, and some didn't want to even think or talk about it. If they were one of those marching, the memories were often too traumatic to recall, or they had simply blocked them out and could remember nothing. And if they were watching on the sidelines, their inaction was now something that weighed heavy on their mind, too. Many thought it was just better to put it all behind you and move on. She thought that, too, except when it came to Gyorgy. She just couldn't get past missing her brother and the not knowing where or how he was.

Increasingly, the Soviets wanted to silence any survivor stories, too. Moscow had been happy to show films of what its own soldiers had discovered at Auschwitz; the victims, the gas chambers, the piles of human hair, because it showed that fascism was the enemy we should all fear. But relatives of those still missing with their claims that their family members might be involuntarily working for the state should stay silent in case concerns were raised.

There could be no criticism of how communism was treating its newest conscripts, who were toiling for an ideological future they weren't even asked if they wanted. Not unless you wanted to become one of the inmates yourself, of course.

While reuniting families scattered by the war was far more difficult that many had imagined, actually moving on without a missing loved one was far harder, even at a practical level. Property could not be passed on, widows could not remarry and children could not be officially adopted if there was no proof of the death they must assume. It was a legal no–man's–land. Confusion and tragedy was everywhere, children found themselves bewildered by the biological parents they barely remembered trying to claim them back from the German kidnappers they now thought of as their mother and father. The young left in orphanages could not remember their real names or anything from their past lives to be able to give any clue as to where their relatives might be. Without living family to seek them out, some disoriented survivors had no one to search for them, to let them know they were loved and missing. Izabella was glad that she had not had Marta before the war, and had to face the horror of being separated and then searching a whole country for her.

Because of this confusion, these loose ends and the endless possibilities both good and bad, Izabella could not rest from searching for Gyorgy. She asked everyone she could where he or she had been sent during the war, what they had seen and whom they had met. But many were keen to put what had happened behind them rather than talk about it. The Jewish buried the horror they had experienced and set about shaking off the past, refusing to remain victims. Her younger sister was like this. She married quickly after returning home, choosing someone that was committed to communism. The couple moved to Budapest to start a new life instead of trying to pick up and mend the tatters of the old one. Izabella felt her sister had left without so much as a backward glance at Kistelek. Her sister did not waste her time searching for Gyorgy.

In time, Izabella also decided talking about the war must stop. She no longer shared her experiences of Auschwitz and

Bergen–Belsen, she looked only forwards, too. But Izabella still struggled to come to terms with losing Gyorgy, refusing to believe he was gone, always half expecting to see him struggling down the street towards her, skin and bone, perhaps with a weak arm half raised. Until he was home, she kept his memory alive by talking about him often. A kind older brother to her, he would have been the perfect uncle to Marta, and a help to Lajos running the business.

Yes, she had left plenty of space for Gyorgy into her new life and she hoped one day he would return to fill it.

Chapter 15

Izabella, 1945, Belsen

It was time to go home. It was time to return to Kistelek, to find her family and friends and to put the past behind her for once and for all. Izabella had made up her mind, and today she would tell dear Anna, who had so kindly invited her to work here in her canteen in the village of Belsen, after they had become close while they were prisoners. It was just a stone's throw away from that hellhole of a camp she had been liberated from back in April, but also a world away.

Izabella had spent six months finding herself again, feeling like a human again. She spent her days cooking the meals that were served to both the off-duty soldiers and to the waifs and strays that remained here long after the camp was burned to the ground. There were 150 covers a day to get through, and it kept her more than busy! Many of the customers were ex-prisoners, waiting for the next stage of their life to begin now they were, physically at least, free. Many of those that stayed on seemed lost somehow, unsure as to where to go now and who to be exactly. In some cases, they could not return home, but perhaps some did not want to. Many hoped to be reunited with families, others wanted to emigrate to foreign and, they hoped, kinder lands. But before any of this could happen paperwork had to be completed, due process taken, so they lived in limbo, desperate for a new beginning but struggling to close the door on the past.

However, Izabella knew she was not like them; working at the canteen had given her an almost immediate purpose, a reason to get up and get dressed in the morning and to carry on. It was all too easy to wallow in what had been lost instead of focusing on what there still was and what there could be. Her work had also given her money to save so that she had enough to buy a few simple items that made her feel 'normal', and like a woman, again. These small treasures, like the mirrored pressed face powder compact and the trinket box filled with hairpins, sat alongside the precious red lipstick pressed into her hand by the soldier on one of those first days of freedom. She knew she would keep the casing long after she had worn down the pigmented wax, as a reminder of when her life had begun again.

That first week after the British soldiers arrived, their green felt berets pulled down on the right of their faces, seemed like a lifetime ago now. At first, many of those in the camp had been overwhelmed. Many were too weak even to heed the cries that rung out as the soldiers advanced. They lay in the wooden huts, skeletal and weak, heads barely lifted. Others fell to their knees and sobbed, Izabella saw one of her fellow kitchen workers kiss the boots of a soldier as he came to a stop in front of her, clearly shocked at the filthy wreck of a human in front of him. None of the detainees were able to truly show their relief at being freed; their movements were agonisingly slow and their breathing laboured because of the abuse their bodies had suffered.

She knew that many of the soldiers had been desperately affected by what they had discovered. Men used to the horrors of war, and seeing the worst of injuries inflicted upon their brothers in arms, had openly wept at what they had witnessed when they arrived at Bergen-Belsen. Decaying corpses were everywhere, and the barely living lay amongst them. Prisoners ate the worms they found on the ground as others, their bodies wracked with dysentery, involuntarily opened their bowels nearby. All the while a damp wind blew across the bitter scene.

Now as Izabella served these men, they spoke of endless nightmares where their subconscious flooded their sleeping minds with the stench of death and the hushed silence of the barren camp they were charged with clearing. These were men that said they would never be the same again. She had heard rumours that some soldiers had physical reactions to the mental anguish they experienced, temporary paralysis, restricting them to their beds, so that they could no longer be a part of it all. Some soldiers paid the ultimate price, contracting one of the deadly diseases that were endemic in the camp. A German air raid took one.

Lying 40 miles north of Hanover, the troops had been aware of the prisoner of war camp Bergen-Belsen, of course, and knew that as Allied forces advanced, the Germans had forced prisoners from other camps to march to here. Instead of housing just over seven thousand prisoners as imagined, as new prisoners arrived the numbers swelled to sixty thousand. All exhausted, all diseased and all without any food to exist on bar the daily ration of a 5cm-thick piece of 'bread' made from sawdust and potato skins. By the time the British arrived the vast majority of the camp had diarrhoea, and many had what they called 'spotted fever' from body lice, their bodies weak with high fever and covered with angry red spots. Pools of vomit and excrement lay all around.

The soldiers found the sheer number of prisoners held at Bergen-Belsen and the vast heaps of dead bodies both devastating and overwhelming. The greyness of the frigid landscape with its rutted mud, coils of barbed wire and emaciated ghostly prisoners in ragged striped uniforms lodged in their minds forever. An oppressive haze lingered over the camp as the men tried to bring relief. Not that they knew how, their training had not covered this.

Their first job was to empty the huts of dead bodies, but even this was a difficult task, the foul odour turning their guts as they tried to discern between the dead and those that very nearly were. The task of bulldozing corpses into mass graves was not one they found easy either; knowing that these people had already been victims of a lack of humanity the scale of which was hard to believe. However, it was essential that the dead were buried to prevent any further spread of disease. The soldiers made captured German soldiers help with the task of bringing out and burying the thousands that had perished at the camp, perhaps hoping to see just an ounce of regret for the crimes that had been committed here.

Despite the best efforts of the armed forces, thousands more prisoners died within those first few weeks, too, their bodies already too far gone with malnutrition and disease. There was nothing you could do but watch these people die, even the medicines they dispensed could not help them. But at least they died knowing that they were free, treated now as a person not a number, given a little dignity and a bed for their final sleep. Not that that helped the soldiers accept the deaths, which numbered maybe 500 a day, any more readily. And most of these people were like Izabella, imprisoned simply for being, or even just looking, Jewish.

Each new day, however, the soldiers would rise to help evacuate the survivors from the unspeakably unhygienic conditions. The soldiers found themselves speaking in half a dozen different languages as they tried to help everyone deposited here.

Putting in a water supply was a priority to enable the 'human laundry' to be set up. Surrounded by trestle tables, inmates would be washed, hosed and deloused. To actually wash and dry herself again with scented soap, hot water and towels became an experience Izabella could never get enough of.

After that first wash, the discarded rags of clothing the former prisoners had worn would be burned and they would be given new clothes, commandeered from the shops in town or gathered from the storehouses of stolen items the Germans had garnered. As they shed their old camp clothes, it was a way to begin to shake off the life they had endured. Later when these people were strong enough they could also help themselves to whatever they wanted from the clothes store affectionately called 'Harrods'. A huge hall filled with spare clothes and shoes, more than enough for them to enjoy choosing what they actually liked. It was one of the little steps back on the road to being themselves again, as an individual with an opinion that mattered.

A dispensary was quickly formed, and it handed out essential medicines to thirteen thousand frail patients a day. If you were able to walk unaided you were considered well. It was a peculiar measuring stick that could have only existed here, at this time.

Another large task was to distribute food to the starving. It soon became clear that it wasn't safe to distribute the meals freely; many died as their stomachs tried to cope with the sudden abundance of succor. Tragically it took these deaths for everyone to realise that the supplies must be watered down and given slowly. All sorts of food was mashed up together, like corned beef and sausages, and then boiled water was added so a thin stew could be prepared. In this way, people's bodies could adapt to eating again at a pace they could manage. Those too ill to eat at first, or those unable to remember how to even swallow food, were ironically more likely to survive than those that rushed at the food in the first few days. Eventually the army distributed four thousand meals twice daily.

And then there was the day of the lipstick. How it arrived no one knew, but many suspected the British Red Cross arranged the delivery, as it seemed to coincide with its arrival in the relief effort. Of course, many of the soldiers were confused by and even cross at the delivery, wondering what on earth lipstick could offer the camp. They would rather have had medicine or food.

But the women of the camp understood. They had spent the last few years being degraded at every turn, their home and countries occupied, driven into ghettos, herded like animals, transported like cattle. Separated from those they loved, robbed of their possessions, stripped and sorted. Told when to stand, sit, talk, eat, work, sleep.

At the camp, the guards had sought to humiliate the inmates. Making them stand for hours on end at roll call, despite their weak bodies. But by simply applying this scarlet flash of colour across their lips the women began to feel human again. Barely clothed, with blankets over their shoulders to protect them from the biting weather, Izabella knew the women clutched this gift with joy because it proclaimed that they were more than just the number carelessly tattooed on their arm.

She understood too, that at the time being politely offered anything, be it a lipstick, a towel or a piece of crockery, meant that you were seen as a person again. The kindness of a gift, and your right to accept it, or not, made you feel human again. After years of her mind being blank, merely existing and surviving, Izabella was aware that she could think of herself as a person, a 'me', once more. Although she would never forget her given number, she began to believe that she was something other than G/01848154.

American soldiers came to help with the liberation too. These big, tall men had accents that sounded like they were from stories Izabella had listened to on the radio. They brought Camel cigarettes and chocolate, and shared their clothes. They were always a lot of fun at the canteen, getting to grips with the Hungarian food she cooked. Louder than the British troops, they would often break into song and try to sweet talk the ladies.

It was easy to feel close to the soldiers that worked to dismantle Bergen-Belsen; they alone understood what had happened here. On the day the memorial was erected, Izabella knew the soldiers were as pleased as the prisoners to see the dirty wooden huts that had been home to such despair razed to the ground with fire. There was a parade to celebrate their triumph over adversity. There was so much hope, although tears were shed too as the people thought about what they had endured.

And after the dead were buried, the people were evacuated and the camp burned to the ground, the recovery could begin.

In place of a concentration camp, the allies created a displaced person camp. Here you could begin to trace your family and consider your options, perhaps even apply to move to Eretz Israel (the land of Israel). And very quickly, as if in defiance of the Nazis and their supporters, a social and cultural scene sprang up there too. Plays, schools, libraries and even newspapers were set up and everyone was keen to make up for the years they had lost.

Of course, not everyone adapted well. The trauma was too much for many. They could not shift the feelings of loss, anguish and emptiness they felt just because they had new clothes to wear and a mattress to sleep on. As they began to recover, they realised they had no place to go, no homes or family to return to, perhaps no village community left to rejoin. They knew only too well that the anti-Semitism they had faced would not disappear overnight because the Germans had lost the war. They could not forgive the people that had stood by as they became outcasts.

Yes, it took a lot to reinvest in life but Izabella had decided to become one of the survivors and start living again.

She was buoyed by the enthusiasm she saw in the camp. From nothing, the survivors quickly began to rebuild. She was not alone in knowing that she was now a widow. Many sought new relationships to replace those they had lost, and became close to the new friends they made having a deep understanding of each other's recent past. Weddings were commonplace, and a joy for everyone to take part in. It was a time of celebration.

Izabella happily chatted to the soldiers she met, of course. One had even asked her to follow him home to England, pressing his spectacles awkwardly up the bridge of his nose as he offered to help, however, he could. She also made friends with the men that had been in Bergen-Belsen, but no one had caught her eye enough for her to abandon the idea that she might one day be reunited with her family. Her goal was simply to return home.

Many were keen to re-establish the Jewish traditions they had been forbidden from observing, others wanted to make sure their opportunity to have a family didn't pass them by. They were keen, too, to grow their community in defiance of those that would have seen it wiped out of existence altogether. As a result of this, hundreds of new babies were born each month in the displaced persons' camp.

Everyone begged the soldiers to tell the world what had happened at Bergen-Belsen, to share their first-hand accounts of what they had witnessed as much as they could. Izabella, however, was not sure she wanted to talk about her experiences over and over again. It had not been easy for her to accept what had happened here, and after her liberation she had faced some dark days confronting both her grief and rage, and even guilt that she had survived while others had not. She knew many former campmates that could not get past this despair and that it would affect them for the rest of their lives.

Instead she locked her memories away and decided she wouldn't speak of them, concentrating instead on her revival. Life was ahead of her, she reasoned, and the past must remain just that.

Chapter 16

Marta, 1979, Manchester

With the terraced shop fronts of Barlow Moor Road behind her, Marta turned into the more residential Elms Road. She would soon bring her car to a stop, parking on the corner of Queenston Road in front of one of the many grand Victorian townhouses, close to the red brick Sha'are Hayim synagogue. It was a journey of just ten minutes or so and when she reached the projecting wings and porch of the synagogue she expected to see a modest crowd gathered to greet the funeral cars; some might join the *levayah* then, while others would stay. The process of mourning would start only after the funeral, and she had recently learnt that in an Orthodox household the females of the family would stay at home to mourn in private once the Rabbi had torn an outer garment of the mourner. There would be no flowers and cremation was forbidden.

Marta knew this final view of the deceased would help bring the closure she found she needed after performing *Tahara*. This was her routine now. Those that had worked with the body alongside her would also come to pay their respects, although they would all take care to remain unnoticed, ensuring the bereaved family was unaware of who in the community had performed the essential ritual for their loved one. After all, this was a *mitzvah* done without an expectation of acknowledgement or gratitude, viewed as the ultimate kindness, because the dead cannot repay you for your service. Neither should their relatives feel indebted.

Marta felt honoured to be one of those selected for the synagogue's *Chevra Kadisha*, the 'holy society' called upon to perform *Tahara*, purifying the body for its final journey. There were about fifteen people from the synagogue's community that might be asked to perform this ritual and, since they often needed to fit in the process at short notice, a few people would need to be called to see if they could make it. Typically they were older, so that they had some life experience and it was likely that they were retired or may be working for themselves so that they could be so readily available.

Tahara was one part of the Orthodox synagogue's work Marta felt she understood. She was not a regular attendee, she didn't read Hebrew and wasn't keen on many of the strict rules; like women not wearing trousers, for example. She felt more than a little judged here, particularly when she attended and saw many of the other women dressed up and wearing big hats at the services. But since it had been necessary to move to Manchester for her second husband Jack's job, she'd willingly joined the Ladies Guild of the *Sephardi* synagogue he was a member of and was happy to help as she could, putting out the cakes and fruit for *Kiddish*. She liked to keep busy.

Marta had known her first marriage was over after a carelessly callous remark Peter threw at her as she lay in a hospital bed. At the time she was recovering from a tumour removal, having at first thought her discomfort was pregnancy. For her husband, the tumour and the doctor's suggestion that Marta's entire womb may need to be removed meant nothing more to him than a great way to lay to rest Marta's desire to start a family. 'Well if you need a hysterectomy at least you won't nag me about having children anymore,' Peter had said. Marta felt like she'd been stabbed in the heart. In that moment she realised her health meant nothing to her husband, and neither had his earlier promises of starting a family.

Initially they had agreed to wait until they were financially secure before having children. But when after five years of hard work towards 'the future' Marta broached the subject of getting pregnant, there were pleas to wait just a little longer. Several more years passed, and in the pit of her stomach Marta knew Peter really did not want to have the children she thought they had planned together. She had packed and left but when Peter asked for a second chance and that they could try for a baby, she trusted all would be well. When her period didn't come, Marta was delighted she would become a mother but her excitement changed to horror when it was found a tumour rather than a baby was growing inside her. Then her husband's lack of compassion at her bedside had proved to Marta for once and for all that her marriage was over. All that was left for Marta was to plan how and when she would leave.

Newly separated, Marta had then met Jack while they both worked at Marks and Spencer. He was a *Sephardi* Jew. His father was from Manchester and had a textiles background, while his mother was from Morocco. His parents had moved to Japan, where they had a *Kosher* wedding, where Jack had been born. But when the country expelled all foreigners, the family settled instead in Egypt. Consequently, Jack had spent a happy childhood in the Middle East with local nannies to adore him, being sent off to an English boarding school when he was 12, and merrily spending his holidays in Manchester with his beloved aunts.

But her time in Manchester had not been so pleasurable. She'd long since left behind her senior buyers job at Marks and Spencer, when even the idea of returning after the birth of her twins had been impossible. But here in this new city she'd been unable to find another job that suited her level of skills yet still allowed her to see enough of her daughter Sarah, now 2 years' old. Sarah's sibling, Esther, had lived for just three days. While still in hospital Marta had realised something was wrong with her baby, but the ward was understaffed and busy because of the Queen's Silver Jubilee. Instead, Marta was written off as a hysterical mother and her pleas for help went unanswered. Esther had an inoperable condition and died. It was the worst time in Marta's life, and she had found no comfort in religion then either, as the Orthodox Rabbi classified her child's death as a miscarriage because the baby was under six months old and sadly her husband followed his lead.

The city of Manchester, too, was suffering, reeling from a sustained IRA bombing campaign. Terrorists had detonated devices in shops and at the Magistrates Court in 1973 and 1974, and planted a bomb that injured twenty-six people outside the Lewis's department store the following year. They'd even been a shooting outside an Indian restaurant in Rusholme. Marta found it a lonely place and wistfully remembered her busy social life in London; here the only people she met were those connected to Jack's new job at Brentwood Brothers. She wheeled the pushchair to the village endlessly, but there wasn't even a café to pass the time in. Thank goodness for Jack's two industrious aunts who still lived nearby, running their luxury lingerie business. They were always so warm and welcoming when she visited with Sarah. She would soon have a second child and knew this baby would be similarly welcomed and loved.

Then she was asked if she would consider extending beyond the duties typically given to the Ladies Guild and become part of a team of people that performed *Tahara* as needed. She had immediately agreed, despite having never seen a dead body, even Esther's. Although she had not been brought up as a practising Jew, she knew a little about the custom already, that strict procedures were followed and that you would only prepare bodies the same sex as yourself. But still she wondered how she would react that first time when she went along simply to observe.

In fact, she found to her surprise that she was neither scared nor saddened by dealing with the dead. There was a special room at Leeches, the undertakers, where the body would already be placed on the table for them. Dressed in surgical gowns and wearing two sets of medical grade gloves, they would first wash their own hands and ask the deceased for forgiveness. Then the women would begin to uncover each section of the body in turn. A showerhead on an extra-long hose enabled the ritual washing, while a hoist allowed the women to move the body easily as they washed and dried the person. The team would fix the hair and nails of their charge and finally dress them in white clothing. One of the older, more experienced, ladies in her 70s would gently sing Hebrew songs as Marta and her colleagues worked, and Marta was comforted by the soft tones that the women sung in.

The sleeves and legs of the clothing would be closed but not knotted and when the body was finally ready it was placed into the coffin. Prayers would be said and some soil from Israel would be added to the coffin because the sanctity of this special land was said to help the atonement of the soul. Then finally the group would call the undertaker to close and lock the casket. It was the custom to sit with the coffin until it was time for the funeral to take place. Occasionally this meant an overnight vigil in an anteroom by a male family member, but since it was mostly arranged for the preparation to take place as close to the burial as possible this was unusual.

For Marta the experience was humbling; it was both peaceful and serene, and she felt almost in a daze during the process. She was often unaware of the time that had passed as the women carefully turned the body on each side to wash it. She found that it was neither a complicated or mysterious process, just a simple act of kindness carried out with dignity. She began to feel that she, too, would like this treatment when her time came, even though, with a family that had been persecuted for its Jewishness, her faith had not been a significant part of her life before this.

Already after moving to Manchester the family had begun to celebrate *Shabbat* and now they had dinner on Friday evening with the appropriate candles and wine. She would also visit the synagogue for major festivals such as *Yom Kippur*.

As she stood watching the hearse draw slowly past the synagogue, she realised she was really only now learning about being a Jew at the age of 32. She had known she was Jewish as a child, of course, not least because of the spiteful things some people had said. Her father was also buried in a Jewish cemetery that her mother visited each Sunday with her and her brother. There had also been the gifts from American relatives with seemingly exotic but Jewish items like *matzo*. Marta and her brothers had taken the sheets of cracker to school to trade for chocolate, a far more delicious treat, they thought. But these Jewish foodstuffs sent by well-meaning relatives often sat side by side on the table with items such as ham, since food was food to the desperate Hungarian at that time. And growing up with a Catholic stepfather and a mother that no longer cared to be reminded that being Jewish had cost her so much, including the loss of freedom, dignity and loved ones, meant they had not celebrated Jewish festivals or been taught the prayers, stories or history of their people. In fact, Izabella's past was never mentioned at home.

When she lived with her aunt in London she had become more aware of how a Jewish community worked together. While Aranka only attended the local synagogue on special occasions and was not a member of one, they had lived among and socialised with other Jewish Hungarians and Germans, raising money for less fortunate Jews. Aranka's good friend and business partner, whom she spent most of her time with, was married to a Jew and that had been the starting point of their deep friendship. Aranka had, of course, left Vienna for London before Europe changed forever, and in London was free to be as visibly Jewish as she wished.

But now Marta took time to think about it, she realised that the Kistelek synagogue had closed when she was very young both because the war had depleted the number of Jews living there and because the communists had banned religion altogether. She thought back to her kindly Catholic neighbours and finally connected the dots. Those bright, gifted Kiss children had worked so hard to get into university, being refused time and time again, because they were fighting prejudice based purely on their religious upbringing. She, too, had struggled to get a place in further education despite her good grades. Even when she'd visited her home town to obtain proof she was Jewish to enable her to get married to Jack in a synagogue, the synagogue's last serving president had been incredulous, truly believing as he told her that 'no one gets married in a synagogue anymore'. Marta saw now that he had lived in ignorance of the world beyond the Iron Curtain, because there in Hungary the freedom to believe and worship as you chose was not a viable option if you wanted to work or study, and eat and live.

A small spark started in Marta. She knew now that her family had endured more than she had ever been allowed to understand. The trauma and lived history her parents had pushed deep down inside them was just beginning to rise to the surface.

Chapter 17

Lajos, 1952, Szeged

Lajos watched Izabella as she walked down the ward, out into the corridor beyond and away from him. He wasn't sure if he would see his wife of six years again but he knew that she would be okay without him by her side, and that she would take ferociously good care of their young children, Marta, now aged 5, and her younger brother Gyorgy, aged just 3. He knew this because Izabella, like him, was a survivor and together they had always vowed that they would rise again in defiance of all those that would see them put down. And they had.

He thought of Marta and how she loved to sit on the steps of the family shop, chatting to everyone that went in and out. He hoped her ankle would heal from the motorbike incident, boy had he got in trouble with Izabella that day! He had sat his daughter on it as a bit of a joke, but she'd pressed her leg on some hot metal.

Gyorgy, of course, was so little, a robust toddler with a shock of dark hair. He doubted if his son would be able to remember him as he grew up, but how he loved to see his family laugh and play and rest beneath the chestnut tree in the yard as he walked back and forth from the shop to the storage area just beyond. He hoped the children would come in time to know another father, a decent man that would provide for them and his wife after he was gone. He didn't want them to miss out on anything good life could bring. Lajos and Izabella talked often about their hope that the children would be able to access education and secure decent jobs and, one day, travel overseas, where their lives could perhaps be safer from the social upheavals they had endured. They dreamt of a place for Marta and Gyorgy that was far away from both fascism and communism, and from those that would use these ideologies against the people. He wondered if there was such a place? Could Jews ever really be safe?

Lajos struggled to admit it but it seemed his health was finally failing him. He had been in and out of hospital so very many times in the last two years that he had lost count of the many visits he'd made. He felt weaker each day he lay here, rallying only when Izabella visited him, which she did without fail every other day, making the 60-kilometre round trip on the motorbike they shared. His wife left their children with Piri, who acted as their nanny when necessary as her mother, Franciska, helped out in the shop and the house alongside Izabella.

As was her way, Izabella had not told Marta and Gyorgy the severity of their father's illness this time. Like him, she believed that the children should be protected from the worst of life. 'What help would worrying about a future without their father be to the children?' she had said. Life was simply the challenge you woke to every day, dealing with it as best you could, one hurdle after another. His illness had seen him slowly withdraw from hands-on parenting as he had spent more and more time sick in bed. He hoped his children would not grieve too badly.

In the end, it was his time at the labour camp that was to be the death of him after all, but not in the way he had imagined all those years ago. It made Lajos so angry that overcrowding in ghettos and camps, lack of sanitation, inadequate nutrition and absence of medical treatment meant typhus decimated so many of his people. The policy of deliberate neglect had been just an economic and indirect way of killing off those the Nazis and Arrow Cross regarded as vermin. He had fought off the often-fatal, lice-borne bacterial disease once, but the damage it left behind had caught up with him. His heart had been weakened by the years of mistreatment, and it was now vulnerable to infection like the rest of his body.

This illness was really just the continuation of the compromised health he'd battled since the war ended. Two years ago in August he'd been hospitalised with a dangerously high temperature as sepsis ravaged his organs. Horrified at his general health, the doctors told Izabella that his liver was swollen, his kidneys infected and that he was anaemic. They prescribed penicillin and six months' bed rest, perhaps being justifiably horrified at the state his body was in. Even his teeth and tonsils showed the years of abuse he'd endured.

Lajos knew he hadn't been the best patient then. He'd been restless and refused to stay in bed. He had argued with his wife about taking it easy time and time again, Izabella had even threatened to leave him, begging him to consider her and the children if he was to kill himself with the exertion. It had been hard to accept his limitations because the very opposite behaviour had saved him in the past. Defined him even.

At first he could barely get to the bathroom unaided, Izabella had to lead him there, weak as a kitten, but early in the New Year he'd turned a corner and by the summer he'd put on some weight. They'd had a family photo taken then, to capture this hopeful moment when there were all safe and well together. But the discomfort had still kept him up at nights, so he and Izabella often sat up talking away the hours instead. Maybe he hadn't recovered after all.

This year, however, had extinguished their hope of a healthier future. By February the doctors were operating on his stomach and he hoped this would bring relief, but by spring both his legs had swollen from the tops right down to his feet, and walking became impossible. Reluctantly, and on Izabella's insistence, he'd come back into hospital in June ready to accept treatment. But eight weeks later the doctors told him and his wife that it was too late and there was nothing more to be done. It had been impossible to take in that this was a battle that they couldn't and wouldn't win together.

On his instruction, Izabella had written to his sister, Aranka, in London. He had done so before but was unable to write much then, and now, he was even less able. Izabella had asked Aranka to come and visit, but she hadn't been entirely truthful about how serious it was, as Lajos had asked her to spare his sister the worry and pain still. Aranka, of course, hadn't been able to visit. It wasn't easy to get in, let alone get out of, Hungary these days. Aranka had been lucky to leave for Vienna when she had, and because of her marriage and hurried escape to England her life had taken a very different course to his. He was pleased his beloved sister had escaped the persecution he had faced over and over again. He was pleased she hadn't suffered in the ghetto like his mother, or perhaps worse, being young and healthy, survived the ghetto but instead reached Auschwitz.

Although he had known he was ill, the terminal diagnosis had still come as a blow, sucking from him entirely the optimism he usually had. Now he worried about the family business, nationalised in April by the communists, with the doorway between the shop and their home roughly bricked up. Izabella worked there still as a state employee for a pittance. The indignity! The brass neck of these communists – to take away the business and then reduce its owner to a slave existing on a miserable wage. He was angry and he was anxious. Angry that everything they had worked for had been taken from them, and worried that his wife would struggle after he had gone. Even though Izabella was one of the most resilient people he had ever met, would she be able to carry on against the force of communism? It was a regime that regarded her as bourgeois and in need of humiliation. It was a regime that would ensure, too, that their children would pay the price of their parents' former success. As if they hadn't earned every single thing they now owned from hard work alone. After the war he had been reduced to literally nothing.

It was now September and everyone was urging him to go home to his family for these last precious days. He refused, telling Izabella he'd rather die in the hospital and spare her and the children the pain of watching him suffer. Far better he thought that everyone remembers me in better times. He knew it pained his wife to see him in this hospital bed struggling to breathe. He couldn't walk, but he couldn't lie down in comfort either. He waited for the relief the afternoon administration of his dose of morphine would allow him. Still Izabella had begged him to allow her to arrange an ambulance to bring him home, but he wouldn't relent. He knew his time was close now.

He knew too that he had chosen the right woman to marry. He loved Izabella with all his heart, despite the fact he may not have shown it that well. He had left it late to marry, so keen to build up his business with his dear mother, so focused on expanding into new areas like radio. He had his own business by the time he was 20, and contributed to the village council. He was well liked at the synagogue and among the businessmen of Kistelek.

But he also understood the world outside Hungary. The war had begun when he was 35 and since then he cleared many hurdles where lesser men had fallen. Everything he and his mother had worked on had been swept aside by politics and power. But Izabella had helped him recover and rebuild his life after the war; she had been there every step of the way, feeding him, loving him and bearing his children. Together they drew a veil over the past and vowed to move on with their future together. He treasured every last moment he could spend with her.

Lajos Seiler died at 1.15am on 20 September 1952. He was aged 48. His body was one of the last to be buried at the Jewish cemetery in Kistelek, where it remains today. On his tombstone Izabella had the following words inscribed: 'Time forgets everything, but the memory of you will live forever.'

Chapter 18

Marta, 2002, Manchester

Marta heard the snap of the photographer's camera as she accepted the Queen's gloved hand and performed the customary curtsy. And, always one to notice personal style after years in the fashion trade, Marta admired how Her Royal Highness looked classic yet bright, her berry lipstick matching the shining jewelled broach pinned high on her left shoulder. Her majesty was dressed in a simply-cut collarless lilac coatdress and co-ordinating hat that boasted a generous brim. She also wore three strings of pearls at her neck, and more of the precious stones at her ears, yet had a look that remained understated and timeless. She was grace personified.

Marta herself felt uncomfortably hot in her wool knit suit, partly because Manchester was enjoying an uncharacteristically warm day and also because of the nerves afforded by the occasion itself. As distracted as she was by the fabric of her electric blue jacket that she had chosen so carefully that morning clinging to the back of her neck, Marta was able to enjoy her surprisingly easy conversation with the Queen, who asked friendly questions and seemed genuinely interested in the answers she received. All the while though Marta was studying the monarch's flawless complexion. It was clear the Queen wasn't young, and yet the natural open smile sat on an unbelievably age-defying face. It was not something Marta would forget.

Marta's time with the Queen was over and she was relieved that she had remembered to follow the correct protocol, using 'Your Majesty' at first reference and then 'Ma'am' to rhyme with 'jam', just as they had been briefed by the palace staff. As the Queen was guided away from her and towards the *Bima* at the centre of the synagogue where she would be shown the open *Torah*, Marta felt her shoulders relax.

The bespectacled *Sofer Setam*, the specialist calligrapher in charge of writing and caring for the scrolls, would now explain how they had been written in the same way since Moses had created the first *Torah* scroll in 1312 bce. From her days working as a guide, Marta knew there was plenty to tell the Queen about the scrolls.

For example, the *Torah* would always be written by hand, with a quill pen and ink, on specially prepared parchment known as *Klaf*. Many pieces of *Klaf* would then be stitched together to make the long roll required. It was not a job for the faint-hearted as a *Sofer* must know more than four thousand Judaic laws before he even started, and any mistakes in the lettering could mean starting the entire work all over again. The precious scrolls were kept in the ornate *Ark*, often covered in silk or velvet, and when they were opened and read on the *Bima*, rather than touching them, readers used the silver *yad*, a pointing device with a delicately moulded miniature hand with an outstretched index finger, to do so. The visitors loved that little hand!

It was details like these that their visitors found fascinating, indeed Marta herself had learnt much about her religion through volunteering here. It was funny how the political history of Hungary had prevented her from learning about Judaism as a child but that she was now learning so much as an adult here in Manchester. And it was quite by chance really.

Of course, it was an unbelievable honour for the museum to be chosen as one of the locations that Queen Elizabeth would visit on her Golden Jubilee tour. It would have been difficult to choose one of the many synagogues in Manchester above another, and so the museum offered the perfect way to meet representatives of the faith, without offending some sections of the community. It was a fortunate gift!

Marta breathed a deep sigh as she realised that finally the Orthodox Jews and the Jewish press would take the museum and its work seriously. Since there was no greater *mitzvah*, or blessing, than being in the presence of a ruler, the pavements of the perpetually busy urban road outside were today crammed with the more conservative members of their faith, vying to see and be seen. The sea of covered heads and modest clothing stretched a mile down the street.

Initially Bill Williams, a founding member of the Manchester Jewish Museum and a lecturer at the city's polytechnic, had welcomed the Queen as she'd approached the museum. While Bill wasn't Jewish, he was an important figure in the acknowledgement of the role Manchester Jews played in the community. It was he who had put the time into tracing the history of those Jews that had settled in the city, along the way saving many important records of the achievements and contributions they had made. His vision was of a museum that would be welcoming to all, showing and sharing universal experiences through the stories of one particular culture.

In turn Bill had introduced Basil Jeuda to the Queen. Basil stood a full head and shoulders above her majesty and had to subtly lean both in and down to talk with her, his hands clasped neatly behind his back, his deep purple *kippah* clearly visible. He was the current chair of the trustees that were bringing to life the idea of educating people about the Jewish religion, and it was his job to escort the Queen into the interior of the museum, where on his way he introduced Marta and another key trustee, Melvyn Flacks, who was also a friend of Marta, as they were both stationed at the door.

Just before the Queen had arrived a sudden hush had descended on everyone within the building's interior and, as if all under a spell, the gathered crowd rose as one towards the ceiling and its stunning Victorian sunburners at the precise moment she entered.

It had certainly been a long journey from the initial idea to where the institution found itself today, thought Marta. The idea of turning the synagogue into a museum had been a response to the Jewish community gradually moving out of the Cheetham Hill area, and needing a synagogue closer to their new homes to abide by the rule of not driving on *Shabbat*. But what would become of the beautiful building that would be left behind, people had asked? Built initially by *Sephardi* Jews in 1874 it was a stunning reflection of the origins of the community, decorated with Moorish Islamic architectural motifs.

By 1982 the congregation had happily moved to a more convenient new synagogue on Moor Lane in Salford. Meanwhile, the Jewish Heritage Committee had formed and raised the funds needed to start on the building work that the old synagogue would need to become a museum. It was a far better alternative than letting the beautiful building fall into a state of disrepair, or be converted into a warehouse or restaurant, a fate that had met several other synagogues nearby.

There was, of course, more than a year of expensive, specialist repair, which included a new roof, and restoration of the large stained glass window. The window had been installed in 1913 as a memorial to the former Synagogue president, Ezra Altaras, and sat proudly over the synagogue's *Ark*. The museum doors had opened in March 1984. What a proud day that had been, thought Marta smiling, with the result of all their hard fundraising efforts there for all to see.

However, even the initial concept had not been without its detractors. The idea of demystifying Jewish customs and beliefs was deemed unnecessary by many, with some arguing that pointing out differences between the Jews and the rest of the community wouldn't help integration. The local *Jewish Gazette* had even claimed in 1978 that Manchester Jewry needed the museum 'like it needed a ham sandwich'. Now it had royal approval however, it seemed opinions had changed. This very special museum visit would garner far more sympathetic headlines now, Marta was sure!

Marta had become involved with the project in the early 1980s, after visiting an exhibition at the Whitworth Art Gallery. The work shown was a collection of pictures drawn by children held at Bergen–Belsen by the Germans; a period of time she knew little about despite her heritage. As she walked through the exhibition the placard she'd noticed at the entrance stayed in her mind. Volunteers were needed to help establish a Jewish museum. Perhaps there had been something fated about the fact Marta found herself there, so moved by the images she saw, at a time when she too was seeking something more in life, a purpose if you like.

As it turned out, showing the wider community that Jewish people were just like them in many ways, and not something to be feared, was that purpose. Now she met with her fellow trustees once a month, often hosting the meetings at her home so that she didn't need to worry about childcare. Along the way these people had become her friends; now celebrating diversity and promoting acceptance was her work.

Marta still recalled the day when a schoolgirl aged maybe 10 or 11 sat crying on the bus parked up outside the building, her teacher trying to cajole her inside the museum where the rest of her class were about to begin their tour. Marta was working as a guide at that point, and she watched as the teacher eventually coaxed this tiny child out. When she eventually entered the building, she clung desperately to her teacher's hand in fear, but by the time she left she was laughing and jumping about. It turns out the child's parents had told her ahead of her trip that Jews eat little Christian children. There was much education work to be done in those days and witnessing this incident reaffirmed the importance of the museum and its hospitality to Marta.

The strong initial uptake of the school visits the museum offered was largely due to the lucky coincidence that the national curriculum was beginning to include the study of minority religions, but since the same teachers booked to come back time and time again, Marta knew the museum was doing a good job of teaching its guests. The exhibitions focused on how Jews had come to find themselves in Manchester, such as those that arrived from Germany as part of the Kindertransport rescue effort. These stories of Jewish migration and settlement in the city made it unique. As well as the school trips, and the gift shop, the museum also hosted Jewish food exhibitions with a mocked-up *Shabbat* kitchen and the opportunity to taste the braided *challah*. In this way, the museum kept its ties to the *Sephardi* Jews that had come here when it was a synagogue, with the Ladies Guild that would prepare *Shabbat* for the congregation coming here to share the same.

In its work to unite the diverse community within which it was situated, the museum also worked with the local Black and Jewish forum, sharing events and cultures. Marta had always been brought up in an open fashion, with a mix of religions in her own home and on her table, and so it felt natural to her to be interested in everyone that she met in this new city. But working with the museum had given her something on a personal level, too.

Up until this point her move to Manchester had made her feel disconnected. She felt as if she was floating about and lacking in purpose, and she found her days unfulfilling. But teaching others about Judaism had brought her a sense of pride in her religion, and even more so, bringing Jewish and non-Jewish people together to help gain an understanding of each other made her feel both competent and confident.

Yes indeed, thought Marta, there is more that binds us together than separates us.

Chapter 19

Izabella, 1973, Budapest

Izabella focused on the top of the wardrobe, its straight, metal edges as harsh as the surroundings she now found herself in. It stood silently opposite her bed and the small table alongside it. All the furniture was made of the same metal tubing; the floor that she so often stared at was grey-blue linoleum. The surroundings were practical, of course, being easy to sterilise but everything was cold to the touch and utterly lacking in any comfort. Even the floor was prone to causing the staff's heavy shoes to make an unnerving sharp squeak as they turned to enter the always-open door that led to the ward beyond.

She shared the wardrobe with the room's other occupant, a lady that seemed to lay virtually motionless in another identical bed placed between hers and the window. Sometimes, if the curtain that now surrounded her bed was momentarily parted, the two women managed to smile vaguely at each other, both sympathising with the other's fate, but mostly they lay there in the quiet, waiting alone together for what Izabella knew certainly, for her at least, was inevitable.

Now Izabella was gravely ill, visitors had been banned. Was it to spare the well-wishers the trauma of seeing their relatives suffer, Izabella wondered, or to protect the hospital staff from accusations of lack of appropriate care. It made no difference anyway; Izabella could no longer fight those that sought to make her decisions for her.

Instead Izabella used her energy to will the pain away, like she had so many times before in her life. Hunger, fear, rage and even physical pain, she knew these were all things you could overcome if you were strong enough.

But there, on top of the wardrobe, in its usual resting place in a white pot was the cream that could offer her some temporary relief from the pain the two colostomy openings brought her. However, if she wanted it to be administered, like every attention received in the hospital, she would have to pay for the privilege. Which is why, after each application of this lotion, the staff member would stand on her tiptoes to make sure to put it back where a dying woman would not be able to retrieve it for herself. Before her kidney had failed, she was able to ring for the nurses' attention and request the cream, but now even that was beyond her. She drifted in and out of consciousness, waking to see only the curtain forever drawn around her bed.

Izabella's thoughts turned to her daughter, Marta, who had recently visited. Marta had wanted to move the cream to where her mother could more easily reach it, so that she could apply it whenever she needed it. But Izabella had known better than to risk angering her caregivers, and so the cream had stayed on the wardrobe. Placed just beyond her reach, like so many things before.

Izabella knew it had been difficult for Marta to hide her shock at seeing her mother. Once she had been a strong broad woman, with a proud physical presence it was hard to ignore.

Now she weighed so little and her clothes were baggy. In the six years her daughter wasn't able to see her, Izabella had faced two operations on her stomach. The first colostomy was hard to bear, but she was told that within six months a second operation would rectify the need for the cumbersome stoma bag. It didn't.

The second operation to reconnect her bowels had failed and proved too much for her body; her kidneys had stopped working while she was on the table. The surgeon in charge had decided not to offer dialysis at the time, for fear of causing a heart attack, too. Now she had two openings on her stomach and was in pain. It seemed she would die not, as she had feared, from the growing cancer inside her but from this untreated kidney failure. The doctors knew it, her family knew it, and she knew it. It was just a matter of time, and she must lie here until then waiting.

Marta had visited after this second operation, when András had told her how ill Izabella now was. Her daughter has said she planned to find a better-quality stoma bag when she returned to England, but Izabella wondered if she could last long enough for her daughter to visit again. Still Izabella had marvelled at her daughter's description of her new country's national health service, where anyone, rich or poor, could visit a doctor and receive free advice and treatment. She knew if anyone could find a better solution it would be her determined daughter, who lived in a land of hope.

Ever considerate, and thinking of clothes, when she came Marta had brought with her to the hospital a beautiful dressing gown for her mother to wear. Of course, it would have drowned the woman she was now, and it would likely have got 'lost' too, so after Marta had left, she had sent it home with András. Nice things were better stored for a later need anyway; after all, you never knew what was around the corner.

What had Marta been talking to the surgeon about when she had been here, Izabella wondered? Had he asked for more money? A gift? It was likely to be something like that, but she supposed she would never know. So many unanswered questions and so many secrets in Hungary still, thought Izabella. She was so glad that Marta now lived in England. It was such a relief to think her daughter would be spared the kind of suffering she had endured, and the bewilderment of never knowing how life might change for the worse on a seeming whim of the authorities.

Marta had not been her only visitor, of course. Her dear András had come every day until he was forbidden to do so. He'd been so cross with the hospital for not giving her the dialysis treatment, and that had spilled over into angry words with the father of Gyorgy's wife, who was a urology consultant at the very same hospital. András was sure this consultant could have convinced the hospital to save her, even though he'd not been working at the time.

Instead, András did his best to find the money they needed to ensure Izabella got the attention of the nurses when she needed; a filled envelope here, a handshake concealing some crumpled notes there. And he would bring whatever she said she wanted to eat, even when it had been only ice cream that she could manage.

Gyorgy had also visited, and brought his daughter, Ildiko, with him. Ildiko was Izabella's first grandchild, and such a charming little thing, blessed with a full head of astonishing curly hair. Her youngest son had also been. He was waiting to start his obligatory military service and while Izabella hated anything to do with army men in uniform, she knew Laszlo must do as he was bid. It had been nice to have her family gathered around her while she could. It had taken her mind off the pain, off the inevitable end point. No one had told her she was dying, of course, but she was not stupid; she knew that even she had her limitations.

She hoped her children and her grandchildren would be happy long after she was gone. She had made it her mission never to unload upon them all that had happened to her. They lived without the burden of the past that Izabella still carried.

First there had been the confusion of being a barely married young woman in a world turned upside down by the politics of hate and division. This man, whom she had really only just began to get to know, was taken off to labour camp while she was ushered first to the ghetto and then Auschwitz. She had arrived there physically strong and with a practical edge from life as a shopkeeper's daughter and yet really she was just a sheltered Jewish village girl, with a traditional upbringing and an arranged marriage. Many like her were murdered immediately, shot by the guards, or worse. Many more simply faded away during the endless internment.

But during her time at the camp she discovered that she was so much more than a victim. She had an inner strength, one that meant she was able to survive all types of terror. The sights, and sounds of cruelty and torture, and the nightmares that came after you had witnessed such things would break the others, but not her. She held on and she survived.

Then there was the march to Bergen-Belsen. Exhausted and barely able to comprehend there was more agony to come, she trudged on and on at the insistence of the guards. She saw people fall and drop, left where they fell, as if they were dead leaves from a tree scattered behind them on an autumn path. But she marched on and she survived.

Liberation came and she rebuilt herself, eventually returning home to be reunited with those that were left. She wore nice dresses, piled her hair into a bun and always applied red lipstick. She remarried and together her and Lajos built a home and began a family. She paid for her camp tattoo to be removed and chose to have a scar rather than memories. She survived.

But fate hadn't finished with her. Life under communism eventually cost her house, her livelihood and her husband, too. She worked harder, found love and married again, became a mother again. She accepted her life and the rules she must follow. And she survived.

But now, she found herself here. Exhausted, small and struggling for breath. She faded in and out of consciousness, aware of the pain, yet helpless to do anything about it. She thought of all she had battled, all she had achieved, the faces that would haunt her but she thought mostly of the faces of those that she loved.

And now she felt she had survived for long enough.

Izabella died from untreated kidney failure following unsuccessful surgery for bowel cancer on 13 March 1973, aged 53. She was cremated and her husband, András Barkanyi, placed her ashes in a columbarium in Budapest Cemetery. When András died, the family bought a burial unit for his ashes and Izabella's remains were moved to their final resting place with him.

Chapter 20

Marta, 2009, Twyford

Marta looked out onto Sycamore Drive. It was mostly a quiet street, although with an infant school and a popular park close by, it could get busy. Her home sat amongst a row of similarly sized bungalows, each with its own patch of well-tended garden to the front. The neighbourhood was friendly and relaxed, people had time to stop and mention the weather, dog walkers smiled as they passed on their way to the Rec, the toddlers headed to and from the nursery close by stopped to admire the daisies and dandelions growing in the grass verge, favourite toy dangling from their hands. She thought how tremendously happy she had been since coming here. She'd not just found a new home, she'd found a community and she'd found a part of herself that had lay hidden, too.

For Marta moving to the Berkshire village of Twyford had been a fresh start. She was closer to both her daughters here, with younger daughter Laura already living in the village, and her elder daughter Sarah living nearby in London. She was a grandmother twice over too now. Sarah had been first with Bertie in 2007, and then a year later, Laura had her first child, a boy she'd named Isaac or 'Zachi' as he was known. Marta was now semi-retired and had plenty of time for granny visits. This balanced well with her continued involvement as trustee of the Jewish museum back in Manchester.

To be in place in time for Laura's May wedding, Marta had moved into rented accommodation first. She had been looking for a house to call her own, but prices locally weren't comparable to Manchester, so the process took some time. Twyford was also such a popular place to live, with its proximity to the vibrant Thames Valley, good schools and fast train to the capital, properties were snapped up quickly. It really was a seller's market then! Eventually Marta had been lucky enough to find a plot of land in the centre of the village, where a fire had devastated a bungalow. It was too small for the big developers to want to muscle in on and rather impulsively she had made an offer without even seeing it. Once it was hers, however, she set to making herself a home, and using her business brain to capitalise as much as she could on the deal.

Marta submitted plans to rebuild the plot, turning it into two semi-detached bungalows rather than one detached home. She hoped to live in one and sell the smaller of the two on. While the building was taking place, the housing market dropped however, and by the time she'd moved in, she instead rented out the second property. That's life, thought Marta; plans made in advance don't always pan out!

After her divorce from Jack in 1995, Marta had realised how much support her *Sephardi* synagogue had offered her and her girls, and her work with establishing and running the museum had given her further cause to embrace her ethnicity. So, leaving nothing to chance, ahead of the move Marta had investigated both of the synagogues local to her new home in Twyford. Goldsmid Road in Reading was home to the county's only Orthodox synagogue, while Maidenhead synagogue was led by Rabbi Dr Jonathan Romain and was a member of the Movement for Reform Judaism. Having already had experience of an Orthodox synagogue, and finding some of the rules too much, she'd opted for the latter and sent off for membership ahead of her move.

It wasn't long after she'd arrived in the village when the Rabbi appeared unannounced on her doorstep. He was 'just passing' of course, although Marta later learned this was very much his MO! Jonathan was quick and eager to find out all about Marta and her background. Looking back now, she realised he'd instantly spotted that her business skills would prove useful to the community. Not much later Jonathan had phoned and asked her if she'd consider running the kosher shop for the synagogue. She'd agreed, of course, but had underestimated the role. Jonathan had described something quite simple; admin, stock control tasks and the like. Marta smiled as she realised she didn't know the half of it when she took it on.

The shop operated from the small, narrow room at the back of the synagogue. There was a small fridge in place already, plus some shelves and a chest freezer. The room opened out on to the car park, which made bringing in deliveries very easy. After placing an order online, suppliers would turn up and unload, with one of the admin staff putting the goods directly into the fridge or freezer as necessary. It was a lovely service to be able to offer the synagogue community.

Marta had never run a kosher home as such; she changed her kitchen equipment at *Passover* yes, but that was about it. She learnt quickly what was needed for the kosher shop though and was ready when the customers came on Sunday mornings, typically while their children attended Sunday school. The shop was also open on a Wednesday, when the synagogue staff covered the sales instead.

Marta ran the shop just as it had been done for a few months, while she got to grips with everything. But pretty soon she'd seen room for improvement. She found the food from the existing fresh deliveries was often wasted as it went out of date so quickly, so she headed into Golders Green in London and found some new suppliers like Carmelli and Menachems. She'd drive into town early on the Sunday morning and be back in time to have *challah* and pitta ready for the eager customers. Freshly baked, these items were really something else to taste and developed a whole new fan base.

Slowly but surely, Marta worked to get better prices so she could pass on the savings to the synagogue's community too. It was just like being back at Marks and Spencer, developing a relationship with a supplier and negotiating a deal. And she'd begun to expand the range of items, too, sometimes goods for the major Jewish holidays that people would order several weeks in advance, and sometimes items that Israeli members missed from their days in Israel. She'd even begun to stock deli items and had Jewish greetings cards that sat in a rotating stand!

Marta needed help from other volunteers now, too, and even an extra car to go and pick up all the orders from London on Sunday. They'd bought a bigger fridge freezer and the shelves were full of basics. Now the shop stocked everything from smoked salmon and frozen meat to ice lollies and *matzo*. The shelves were filled with items with brand names like Rakusens and Osem, and you could have been forgiven for thinking you'd stumbled on a tiny version of London's renowned Kosher Kingdom!

Marta loved her time in the shop. It was a busy, social hub now, and Marta got to know everyone easily. On Sundays they'd be a queue of kids waiting for their Bamba corn puffs and before festivals there was a sense of excitement in the air. The shop brought the whole community together and Marta was right there in the middle of it all. Before too long, she'd doubled, and then tripled takings in the shop.

Marta smiled to herself again; Jonathan had certainly known what he was doing when he asked her to take over. He was a force of nature and didn't mind speaking up either. As well as a mainstay in the Jewish community, he was a well-known writer and broadcaster. In 2003 he'd been awarded an MBE for his work with mixed-faith couples. She was so glad she'd joined the Maidenhead synagogue when she'd moved south.

Marta realised joining the synagogue and becoming so very involved had made her more aware of her Jewishness than she had ever been. It was the first time she felt she had belonged to a community. Being a Jew was who she was. And it was a good thing. When she was growing up saying you were Jewish, following Jewish traditions and being obviously Jewish was not encouraged. That part of her identity had been cloaked in secrets and unspoken fear. And until she started to learn about what had happened in Europe, she had no real idea why. Under communism, schoolchildren weren't taught about the Holocaust. And her parents hadn't mentioned their suffering either.

From her work in the shop she was learning about what was kosher, and what was not, and exactly why that was. She learnt about each Jewish celebration, and the meaning behind the various traditions attached to them. Marta now found she had begun to enjoy the synagogue services, too, and regularly attended on Friday night and on a Saturday. Since she'd never been taught Hebrew, she followed the prayer book phonetically instead.

With more time to call her own here in Twyford, she'd finally re-read her family letters. She'd sifted back through Aranka's carefully catalogued family archive, ready to learn more about what had happened to her mother, her father and the grandmother she was named after. In the past she'd swept such paperwork up and packed it away, unable to process the painful experiences that lay behind the information. But now, with the safety blanket of the community around her, she was ready.

She understood then that when she was younger, the older generation didn't want to talk about what had happened in places such as Auschwitz because they wanted to move on with a future, not stay rooted in the horror of the past.

But those that had survived, those with such tales to tell, had begun to realise that if they didn't speak up their experiences might soon be buried with them. Earlier in their lives, the survivors had tried instead to move on, putting everything behind them, not wanting to dwell on their time as victims, not wanting their experiences to define them. As they became older however, they were faced with the fact that if they passed away and hadn't told of what had happened, nobody would know the truth. And if you don't speak up, doesn't that mean the perpetrators will have gotten away with their crimes for good? And if you stay silent the lessons of the past are lost too, surely? Marta knew that these were the issues that the older members of her community were facing now, it was a case of speak out now, or forever remain unheard.

Through reading the letters, and understanding what it was to be Jewish in that time, in that place, Marta had come to understand how her parents' experiences had impacted the rest of their lives and in turn that of her and her siblings. Marta understood how the twists and turns in life that Lajos and Izabella had faced had formed their personalities, made them into the man and woman they became, and how it had made them the type of parents they had gone on to become. Yes, thought Marta, it has taken me sixty plus years to finally realise how they felt about looking after their family in a world that was never certain, and so often unsafe for them.

Marta now saw for herself how Izabella had never known for sure what was waiting around the corner for her, and that so many times it had been hatred and hardship. So her mother had determined her own daughter should be tough, not mollycoddled. She had never fussed over her daughter or been overly emotional. Izabella wanted her daughter to be strong enough to face whatever life was to throw at her and this was how she worked toward that. Her mother had spent eighteen years thinking that prejudice would come to her doorstep and claim her children, just as it had come for her. It could be in the form of a knock at the door, an official piece of paper or a change of political leaders, and it could come at any time.

Marta understood that it wasn't until she left Hungary that her mother could finally stop worrying about her daughter.

How utterly emotionally exhausting that must have been to live with, thought Marta.

The many letters from her grandmother had shocked Marta the most. A mother, a proud businesswoman, once an integral part of the community, writing desperately to the son she loved not knowing if he was receiving the letters, and later on not really knowing if he was still alive. She wrote about each and every loss. The loss of her business, her home, her carer, her prized possessions, her wealth but the letters also revealed the loss of her freedom, her safety and her humanity. It was with her son she needed to share these troubles. But he too had been taken from her.

Cecilia herself had been rounded up then, alone and vulnerable, her usual protector and shield, her son, miles away, maybe in need of basics such as food and underwear, maybe even worse off than before. Already unwell by this point, she could barely walk to the toilet alone. She found herself a mere number, cramped in a cart, cramped in the ghetto, squashed into a dwelling not designed for its purpose. Full of pain and uncertainty, not knowing who to trust and what would happen next. Clinging to the hope, like those she was among, that they would be taken somewhere better, somewhere to start again. But perhaps also sensing that these people now in charge were not to be trusted. How her grandmother had suffered, and how terrible Marta felt that she had not known this. She felt profoundly sad for the grandmother she had never met, never comforted, but whose pain she now understood.

But, perhaps strangely, Marta found she wasn't angry about her family's suffering. Rather she wanted to make sure that it wouldn't happen again, not to her and her family, not to the Jewish community and not to anyone else either, wherever they were from. She realised anti-Semitism still existed in the modern world, of course. But she also knew that the spirit and self-confidence Zionism has brought to Jews means that they would always fight their corner now. And she was aware that Israel now offered a place for every Jew that needed it.

The modern world was full of good things, democracy in many countries, charitable individuals that were prepared to step in and help those in need. She saw this herself at the synagogue when the community welcomed Syrian refugees, because they understood what it was like to be forced to flee persecution. But there were problems today still, all too familiar ones. There were countries where the population was not free and where the politicians didn't represent the interests of anyone but themselves. This was what worried Marta.

What was important, Marta realised, was that people must learn from the stories of the past, and the lesson should be one of tolerance. What had happened to her family and what was documented in the letters she had rediscovered shouldn't be forgotten. That the same type of hate and cruelty her family witnessed mustn't go unchallenged ever again.

But just how would the messages from her family's legacy be best taught she wondered, and how could she make that happen? She would find a way, she determined.

Chapter 21

Marta, 2020, Harrogate

Her mobile vibrated into life, the familiar ringtone coming bang on the dot of the time the call had been arranged for. So here we are thought Marta, perhaps the start of an important part of the journey for my family's letters.

Letters that were written while their authors struggled with a mix of emotions, including love, sorrow and even desperation. Letters often penned in haste and sometimes in confusion and frustration. Some composed perhaps in a way only the recipient could fully understand what was truly meant by what was said, in case prying eyes were to read them and intrude on personal and private matters and unravel the threads of a secret, a secret buried beneath an indistinguishable chestnut tree in a simple yard, for example.

Letters that were so carefully tucked away and stored they survived both a war and an occupation. Letters that were treasured from the moment they were received. Letters that I, in turn, now treasure and protect, thought Marta. For decades, they have sat silently bundled together waiting to speak out, with me the current guardian of this family treasure trail.

Now she knew her role and the work that her family required of her was to share the letters, their words and the story of the journey they hold with as many people as she could.

Like the rest of the country she was living through what everyone was calling 'unprecedented times'. The seemingly protected modern world was facing a challenge like no other and its name was Covid. In a strange way this virus pandemic was almost like another war or occupation, with but without such clear boundaries. The papers were talking about reigniting the 'Blitz spirit' to help everyone survive, not that my family or I were here then to witness that first-hand, realised Marta. But many miles away, they witnessed the war, internment and so much more, and they saw exactly how resilience works, how it must work if you are to survive.

It didn't seem like that long after the public first heard about this potentially deadly virus that everyone had to get to grips with another new concept, lockdown. And just as the people were asked to, they shut themselves away, often alone, and gave others even a wide berth even when it was necessary to interact to seek out food or exercise. The population covered their mouths with masks and speaking up and out became more difficult. It was surprisingly hard to properly hear and pick up nuances of conversations when you wore a facemask. So slowly, everyone also realised how essential talking is to us all, even the small talk, but perhaps especially the big stuff, thought Marta.

Marta saw how it had been an odd experience that brought a period of introspection to many, too. Suddenly everyone had all this time on their hands – and there was a new focus asking how we could best spend the hours, the days, the weeks, alone in our homes, and make this time valuable. Everyone had to find ways to pass the days of lockdown yes, but more than that everyone also had to find ways to give those isolated days meaning.

Many took the time to reconnect with the people they shared their homes with, but saw surprisingly little of. Telephone calls became necessary again, video calls were all the rage, too. People had Zoom parties and quizzes and the novelty factor of this new way to meet up virtually became a way to compensate for physical separation.

Don't we all just want to make the best of things, even when things are hard? Isn't that what we've always done? Isn't that really what these letters show, too? How to live when it seems impossible to do so? Marta asked herself.

To Marta, the Covid lockdown in the UK seemed to have forced people to ask 'what can you achieve if all other distractions are gone, and you have that most precious of commodities in our modern life; time?' Time, it seems, must be spent wisely otherwise it just slips away.

Well, for me this time seemed to have brought an opportunity and the motivation I needed to press on with reading, translating and sharing the letters that have become so important to me, Marta thought.

A task so easily put off when the world was busy, and just keeping up with her obligations took up all the hours available. She knew it was not an easy task practically or emotionally. She had been careful to photocopy the letters as she worked, to keep the originals that bit safer. At times she felt as if the letters might disintegrate as she handled them and that years of family history could simply run through her fingers and disappear. She didn't want to lose even a tiny fragment of this narrative.

And with the door shut and the world slowed, Marta found she had been able to do so much, read so much, learn so much. Thank goodness for the internet and the phone, all these ways to connect with other people at a distance and a pathway to information and research and records, she thought. There's so much to find once you start digging. And when you start asking the right questions. Brave questions.

Marta had learnt not just about what happened to her family and her parents, all the hardships they faced that they chose not to share and burden her with, but she had also learnt how what had happened to them went on to shape them. How their experiences made them the people they were, and the parents they became. And in turn how the parents they became helped to form her and her life. And these were experiences that somehow reached through all the years that had passed to touch future generations.

We have all inherited their story, their experiences, their learning, and their teachings, Marta realised. Perhaps we have inherited a piece of their trauma, too, however hard they tried to save us from it. Did we also inherit their resilience and wisdom, she wondered? Again, time would be the judge of that.

When Marta first realised the significance of these letters she knew she must keep them safe, preserve them always, just as her father had all those years ago. But rather than tuck them away any longer, and risk them being discarded at a later date, perhaps even by accident as they sit bound in their unprepossessing file, Marta knew she must ensure they are stored appropriately for so much longer. With their intrinsic value officially catalogued and recognised.

When I have translated all the letters to my satisfaction, I will send them to the Holocaust museum Yad Vashem in Israel, decided Marta. What had struck her the most when she visited it herself was the way it dealt with and presented the information it stores and reveals. She recalled how when you visit you could pick a name and then you could follow that individual's experience of the Holocaust around the exhibits and information, making it so much more relatable, personal, real. She wondered if someone would choose a Jewish Hungarian woman named Izabella Tauber? Or a businessman called Lajos Seiler? Perhaps her grandmother, Cecilia, would appeal instead? Would they follow each footstep of her family member's life story? Would they understand their experiences, their emotions, their actions and decisions?

But Marta also knows she wants to do more than just keep this written record of her family safe in a museum dedicated to the Holocaust and the Jewish experience. She plans to spread her family's story to as wide an audience as possible and far beyond those that might seek out such an account. There will be many that would never visit a Holocaust museum, even one as good as Yad Vashem, and many who will never visit Israel, she realises. And she knows if she publishes the letters in just the language they are written in, the audience is restricted further to those that speak Hungarian and also only to those that might choose to read about how a Jewish Hungarian family experienced these painful years.

Marta appreciates the story held within these letters is bigger than just this self-selecting audience. It's not just a story for Jews, for Hungarians or for historians, it's a story about people, and it's a story for people. All people.

Yes, the account covers international events, and well-documented ones at that. But it's also a story of the ordinary lives caught up in these global happenings; her family wasn't well connected then or now. There are no heroics; they did nothing more or less than the many others like them that somehow survived the war as a Hungarian Jew and the occupation of their country by the Soviets. There were simply tangled up in circumstances beyond their control and they got on and lived as best they could.

It's not my story to tell of course, thinks Marta, but it is still my duty to see that it is told, and told to as many people as possible. And so when Laura introduced me to Vanessa, a friend she has made through their children's mutual school I was keen to connect. She is an author with experience in historical non-fiction. Removed from the Jewish experience, and too young to have experienced the war years herself, she will ask the questions an outsider would have. Together we're going to turn everything the letters tell us into a narrative.

Will it work? Will I be able to tell the story of my family to her, and will she be able to set it down into pages and retell it? Will she really listen and see beneath the day-to-day? Can she craft the stories, the clues, the tidbits of information in the letters, and add them to my memories, and my research to make a coherent tale? Will she be able to create a book, find a publisher, breathe air into the story so that it can rise up out of the papers I have before me and be seen? Only time will tell, thinks Marta.

But she knows the first step is to answer the ringing phone.

Epilogue

With a population of over nine and half million, the central European nation of Hungary is small enough so that today you could cross it within just a few hours by car. The capital city, Budapest, sitting in the central region, is now Europe's sixth most popular city to visit. Mainly flat, almost a fifth of Hungary remains covered with forests while three of its ten national parks are UNESCO World Heritage Sites. Foothills, lakes and rivers criss-cross this beautiful nation, which makes it all the harder to imagine this was the place of unimaginable pain and suffering for the Seiler family and so many others.

In 1941 there were about eight hundred and twenty-five thousand Jews living in Hungary. Approximately sixty-three thousand of those people died or were killed prior to March 1944. A further five hundred thousand Jews died under the German occupation thereafter. In fact, less than one-third of Jews who had lived in Hungary in March 1944 survived the Holocaust.[1] Those that died included Izabella's first husband, Erno, who was beaten to death at a labour camp, and Lajos's mother, Cecilia, who by the time she was bundled on to a wagon bound for Auschwitz was too ill to survive the full journey.

Izabella Seiler's greatest pain inflicted by the Holocaust was perhaps the disappearance of her brother, Gyorgy. Although she knew that he had been sent to a labour camp like many men of his age, she received no news thereafter. Without a body to grieve, she could not accept he had died, and her search for her lost brother was never abandoned. It's likely that Gyorgy either died while he was in a forced labour camp, like at least twenty-seven thousand other Hungarian Jewish men[2] and no identifiable records of him existed, or that he became a captive of the Soviet soldiers after the war had ended. Once captured by the Red Army, he was effectively lost without a trace.

It's now estimated that seven hundred thousand Hungarians were taken to the Soviet labour camps, or Gulags as they came to be known. Estimates suggest that around three hundred thousand of those taken never returned.[3] Inmates included civilians and soldiers, and often no distinction was made by the Soviet 'liberators' between the Jewish prisoners and the Hungarian or German soldiers that had guarded them. Later, authorities rounded up anyone suspected of being ethnically German, any dissenting political voices and many others besides, and between the 1930s and the 1950s about fifteen million people disappeared in this manner.[3]

Only since the fall of communism has the existence of these camps been indirectly acknowledged when Russia's parliament adopted a federal law on remedies for victims of Soviet-era repressions in 1991.[4] Sadly this was too late for Izabella to discover if Gyorgy had spent the rest of his life as a captive, missing his family as much as they missed him, or if he lay in an unmarked grave, murdered by the Nazis and their compatriots.

Lajos Seiler survived the brutalities of his work camp, but like many thousands of others, during his time in captivity he contracted typhus. While this bacterial disease is treatable with antibiotics, without medication the death rate for those infected with louse typhus can be as high as 60 per cent. The infection spreads through the bloodstream and can affect the whole body, and for those that survive it untreated, it can bring long-term health effects. This was certainly the case for Lajos, who died in his late 40s because of the lasting damage that was wreaked on his body during his time in forced labour. While his death came seven years after the end of the Second World War, he was nevertheless a casualty of the Holocaust.

Izabella went on to marry again, rekindling her first love with her village sweetheart, András Barkanyi. Having experienced the same upbringing himself, András was a caring stepfather to her children and the couple went on to complete their family of five with Laszlo. A movie script could not have come up with a better happily ever after. However, András was outspoken and his political views meant that the authorities beat and eventually detained him and, just as she had lost her business and home to the regime by nationalisation, Izabella also lost her husband for eighteen months while he was imprisoned without a trial. After his release, András remained under constant surveillance and was only ever allowed to work in menial jobs.

However, as you read this book, I hope it is clear that the Seiler family were far from just victims of the anti-Semitism, the Nazis, Soviet occupation and Stalinism they faced. They were survivors. In fact, what makes the accounts covered within this book so amazing is that the family not only survived against all odds, but went on to build back bigger and better. Time and time again.

Izabella's greatest achievement was perhaps giving her daughter, Marta, the life she knew she herself would never have. Although she did not realise it at the time, when Marta was sent to live in the UK with Aunt Aranka, Izabella was ushering her daughter to a safer, worry-free life. She knew that in England Marta would be able to study, to work, to marry and have a family, wherever and however she liked. She would not need to conceal her identity or watch what she said in public. Of course, Marta had had no idea how the Western world worked when she set off from Kistelek in 1965 and had actually been committed to her Young Communist Group. But perhaps mother knew best and realised once her daughter was free from propaganda and state control, she would see for herself just how much better life would be outside of Hungary.

Marta and Aranka remained close throughout their lives. When Marta's daughter, Sarah, was a baby, niece and aunt saw each other once a week, and later when Marta and her family moved to Manchester, both Aranka and Marta would make monthly visits to each other. While Aranka never mentioned the collection of family letters she had in her possession, Marta thinks she was aware that, as beneficiaries of her will, she and her brother, Gyorgy, would find them. Marta does recall being shown family photographs by Aranka when she was about 18, but like many young ladies, Marta wasn't too interested in people that she'd never met. Aranka went on to live a long and happy life, making it to 91, when she was just as elegant as she had been at 25, Marta recalls. Marta thinks her aunt would have been over the moon to see her mother and brother commemorated in this book.

It's also important to remember Marta and her siblings had a happy childhood, mostly unaware of what was going on politically. They were fed and loved and their parents deliberately did not burden them with the past, lest it affect their future. As well as the packages of clothes and food Aranka sent, once she was able, their aunt came to visit almost every year, and she brought exciting presents and gifts for the children, including a watch for Gyorgy. Aranka happily socialised with Izabella and András, and any of the Jewish community that she knew that were still in Kistelek.

Although as adults Marta, Gyorgy and Laszlo were aware of how their parents were treated, their own lives are testaments to the resilience the family has shown. Like Marta, Gyorgy also successfully left Hungary and lives in Israel, where he moved in 1978. He is now retired and lives with his partner, Ingrid, and between them they have a large family. Gyorgy's eldest daughter, Ildiko, lives in Hungary with her husband, Tamas, and son, Tomi. Marta visits Hungary often and loves to spend time with them. After the death of Marta and Gyorgy's stepfather, Gyorgy dedicated a small woodland in Israel to his memory.

Marta's stepbrother, Laszlo, has remained in Hungary, where he lives with his wife, Anna. He enjoys the freedom to express his opinions without fear of reprisals, travel as much as he wants and live as he pleases in what is now a democratic country, in a way his father was never able to. His own son,

András, has emigrated to the UK and is settled with his partner, Gabi.

Marta clearly remembers Izabella telling her children that they would 'be sorry when you live far from each other' when they fought as children. But the siblings have always remained close, helping each other when necessary, and so she has never had to regret not keeping in touch. The easy and supportive relationship that Marta, Gyorgy and Laszlo have developed and maintained would please their parents immensely.

This book marks an end to several years of emotional work for Marta, sorting, documenting and translating all the letters, photographs and documents that her aunt left behind. We've spent many hours on the phone together using the letters to piece together her family's story.

For Marta sharing what happened to her parents and grandparents through this book is very important. She hopes that generations to come will understand what humans are capable of, and learn not to be afraid to call people out when they cross the line. At the time of writing, we are seeing Russian tanks entering Ukraine, and for Marta this brings back memories of Soviet tanks rolling through her village in 1956 when she was just 9.

The next and final stop for the Seiler family letters will be Yad Vashem, the museum and memorial to the Holocaust in Israel. There the letters will be properly preserved and used to teach generations to come.

The pen is indeed mightier than the sword.

A Message from Marta

My name is Marta Seiler, I am a Jewish Hungarian and have lived in the UK since 1965.

Recently my local Soroptimist group asked me to talk about my faith. Not having any further direction on the subject, I took many hours to decide how I could define MY faith.

In the end I decided that my faith is deeply embedded in the history of my family, the battles they fought simply to BE, to survive.

My early childhood was no different to any other children in my small village. In the first five years my brother Gyuri and I enjoyed the love of my mother, her amazing cooking and hardly noticed that our father was occasionally missing, being in hospital. We had very little memory of him when we started to visit his grave in the Jewish cemetery on Sundays. I do remember when the shop belonging to my parents was nationalised, and the door from my room to the shop blocked up. But to my brother and me it just meant we lost one of our favourite playgrounds.

We attended our small synagogue for a short time before it closed, not that we noticed; at the age of 5 and 3 our priorities were playing with our neighbours and friends mostly on the street or under our wonderful chestnut tree in the garden. Aside from the visits to the synagogue, we had no other reference to religion.

Sometime later, our stepfather arrived, and then our younger brother, Laci. For me, the arrival of a baby was a major point in my young life. I pretended Laci was my baby and for a long time he was the most important person in my life. Many years later, I realised I had left my older brother, Gyuri, out, and I still feel very guilty about this.

Then it was school, being immersed in the teachings of communism, being part of an organisation hailed by the school, the teachers and the custom of celebrating the important dates publicised by our government.

Around that time some children called us names we could hardly identify with, but it sounded like a 'bad' thing to be. This was my first experience of anti-Semitism. I can't remember a lot of explanation by mother, so it was soon forgotten.

The year of 1956 brought changes, our stepfather disappearing for months, being imprisoned for being against the regime. This resulted in the whole family being in the Communist Party's bad books and our mother having great difficulty in getting a decent job.

We children carried on, more or less as before, except with maybe less of mother's delicious food readily available, we survived with food from my father's family's farm arriving under the cover of darkness.

By the time our stepfather returned, I was getting more involved with the Young Communist organisation that I embraced. I often had arguments with my stepfather, quietly, being aware that no one outside our home should hear him express anti-regime opinions.

Judaism only appeared in a strange form at our house at Easter/Pesach time. We received parcels packed with *matzot* from America. It was, of course, sent to be eaten over the festive days in place of bread products. But we also had all the foodstuffs our neighbours had on the table; a joint of ham when there was money for it, cooked eggs and a plate of *matzot*. Gyuri and I managed to take some of the *matzot* to school and exchange it for chocolate, since everyone wanted a taste of the American food!

We never heard of mother's experiences during the war, the scar on her arm was just a scar and it was many years later that I connected it to her experiences in Auschwitz. Like many with the same experience, she simply wanted to forget all about it. The fact that our stepfather was Catholic was only an impression gained by his weekly card games that included the local Catholic priest. Even that just meant that in the winter I was not able to study in the heated living room and had to shiver in my unheated bedroom!

When I left for London at age 18 I knew nothing about religion, certainly nothing of what it really meant to be Jewish. But even today, I know for sure that my absolute tolerance of any religion, colour and different customs came from my upbringing and my experiences in the 1960s.

My discovery of a big box of letters written by my grandmother and my father was frightening.

Every time I was brave enough to read another letter or postcard, I was in floods of tears and I used the excuse of being busy with my daughters, running a business and various volunteer jobs as a reason for having no time to read them, to really understand them.

Living in Manchester, I was involved in the social side of my synagogue and the establishment of the Manchester Jewish Museum. I volunteered as a magistrate and generally busied myself trying to 'repay' my debt for the chances I had in this country. New changes came in 2006–07, including a move, and I found myself a member of the Maidenhead synagogue.

Here was a community where I was accepted. I was encouraged to grow and be my kind of Jew. Here they trusted me to run the kosher shop and in turn my knowledge and understanding of Judaism grew. Here I joined Hebrew classes, then gave them up! I was not pressurised to explain.

This was the community that made me strong enough to properly read the letters, and understand where I came from, who I was, and what purpose the letters could serve.

Before I was to send them to Yad Vashem to be saved, I wanted to publish the story so that there would be another reminder of how savagely men could behave to men just because.

The opportunity came with Covid lockdown, but it was encouraged by my two strokes, which served as a reminder of the constant moving of time.

My relationship with Vanessa was a comfortable one; we had mutual respect. The lockdown served a wonderful purpose since we both had time to concentrate on the project. As I handed over to Vanessa the letters I translated into English,

I was acutely aware that she was spending her time, knowledge and energy without any promise that the work would be published.

I also hope that the book will be translated and published in Hungary, and the story will go 'home'.

Glossary

Ark – The ornate cabinet that holds the Torah scrolls that are used for public worship in Jewish synagogues.

Bima – The raised platform with a reading desk in Jewish synagogues, from which readings are made on the Sabbath and at festivals.

Challah – Special bread usually plaited and typically eaten on ceremonial occasions such as Shabbat and major Jewish holidays (other than Passover).

Chevra Kadisha – A group of specially trained Jews who care and prepare a body for burial.

Gulag – The government agency in charge of the Soviet forced labour camps.

Kiddish – A celebratory meal after synagogue.

Kindertransport – The informal name of a series of rescue efforts between 1938 and 1940 that brought thousands of refugee children, the vast majority of them Jewish, to Great Britain from Nazi Germany.

Kippah – A head covering for Jews, also known as a *yarmulke* or skullcap.

Klaf – A specially prepared, tanned, split skin of a kosher animal (goat, cattle or deer).

Kosher – Foods that conform to the Jewish dietary regulations of *kashrut*, the Jewish dietary law.

Levayah – The Hebrew word for funeral.

Matzo (also matzot, matzah or matza) – An unleavened Jewish flatbread that forms an integral part of the Passover festival.

Mitzvah – A good deed done from religious duty.

Movement for Reform Judaism – Reform Judaism is a religious movement that has modified or abandoned many traditional Jewish beliefs, laws and practices in order to adapt Judaism to the modern world.

Munkaszolgálat – The system of forced labour for Hungarian Jews established by the Nazi-allied Hungarian regime.

Nyilas – The Arrow Cross Party, a far-right nationalist party (in Hungarian 'Nyilaskeresztes Párt – Hungarista Mozgalom').

Orthodox – Orthodox Judaism is the collective term for the traditionalist branches of contemporary Judaism.

Pálinka – A traditional fruit spirit with a high alcohol content, similar to fruit brandy.

Passover – The major Jewish spring festival that commemorates the liberation of the Israelites from Egyptian slavery.

Pesach – Another term for Passover, a major Jewish holiday that celebrates the exodus of the Israelites from slavery in Egypt.

Purim – a Jewish holiday that commemorates the saving of the Jewish people from Haman, as recounted in the Book of Esther.

Sephardi – Also known as Sephardic Jews, Sephardim or Hispanic Jews, are a Jewish ethnic division originating from traditionally established communities in the Iberian Peninsula.

Shabbat – The Jewish Day of Rest, which happens each week from sunset on Friday to sunset on Saturday.

Sofer Setam – A Jewish scribe who can transcribe *sifrei* Torah, *tefillin* and *mezuzot*, of the Five Megillot and other religious writings, also called *sofer, sopher, sofer SeTaM* or *sofer ST'M*.

Soroptimist – Soroptimist International is a global volunteer movement advocating human rights and gender equality.

Tahara – Before a body is buried, it is washed and prepared in this ritual act of purification.

Tahonya – A traditional Hungarian pasta.

Télapó – Literally translated as 'Old Man Winter', this was a way to celebrate Christmas without referring to religion, as communism practised state atheism.

Torah – The compilation of the first five books of the Hebrew Bible; Genesis, Exodus, Leviticus, Numbers and Deuteronomy.

Yad Vashem – Israel's official memorial to the victims of the Holocaust housing the World Holocaust Remembrance Centre.

Yad – a Jewish ritual pointer, popularly known as a Torah pointer. It is used to follow the text during reading from the Torah scrolls and is often shaped like a long rod, capped by a small hand with its index finger pointing from it.

Yom Kippur – The holiest day of the year in Judaism and known as the Day of Atonement.

Hungarian Political Timeline

June 1914
Serbian assassin kills Archduke Franz Ferdinand and Austria-Hungary declares war on Serbia.

August 1914
Britain declares war on Germany, Austria-Hungary joins the Triple Alliance alongside Germany and its allies, to fight the Triple Entente consisting of Great Britain, France and Russia.

April 1917
The United States joins the war against Germany.

October 1918
Former Prime Minister István Tisza is murdered in Budapest during the Aster Revolution.

October 1918
Leftist liberal Count Mihály Károlyi becomes Prime Minister.

October 1918
Hungary and Austria's union is dissolved.

November 1918
Charles IV surrenders his powers as King of Hungary.

November 1918
Germany signs armistice, Hungary faces attacks from Balkan French army and Czechoslovak, Romanian and Serbian governments

November 1918
Southern parts of Kingdom of Hungary attacked by provisional State of Slovenes, Croats and Serbs, with French support Czechoslovak Republic attacks northern territory.

November 1918
Mihály Károlyi is named president of the first Hungarian Democratic Republic.

December 1918
The Romanian Army attacks Hungary's eastern territory, French and Serbian forces occupy the southern parts.

March 1919
Károlyi signs all concessions presented to him by the Entente military representative and resigns. Hungary loses 66 per cent of its pre-war territory.

1919
Communist leader Béla Kun establishes the Soviet Republic, which lasts just four months.

June 1919

Following a Romanian invasion and the collapse of the Kun regime, Admiral Miklós Horthy comes to power, establishing himself as the Regent of the Kingdom of Hungary. The government aligns with the politics of Germany and Italy.

June 1919/June 1920

Treaty of Versailles/Treaty of Trianon formally end the First World War. Hungary becomes a landlocked state with a reduced population and landmass, with many ethnic Hungarians now minorities in other countries.

1938 and 1941

Hungarian racial laws modelled on Germany's Nuremberg Laws established, intermarriage between Jews and non-Jews forbidden, Jews excluded from some professions and civil service.

1939

Hungarian government establishes a forced labour service for Jewish men of arms-bearing age.

1940

Hungary joins Axis powers Germany and Italy, and invades Yugoslavia.

June 1941

Hungary enters the Second World War as an Axis Power, declaring war on Soviet Union.

1942–43
Hungarian units suffer tremendous losses on Eastern Front.
Miklos Horthy and Prime Minister Miklos Kallay recognise
Germany likely to lose the war and Kallay tries to negotiate
armistice for Hungary with the Allies.

March 1944
German forces occupy Hungary, Horthy remains Regent but
Germans replace Kallay with pro-German General Dome
Sztojay, who continues war effort and deports Hungarian Jews.

May 1944
In less than two months, nearly four hundred and forty
thousand Jews deported from Hungary, including those sent
to Auschwitz.

July 1944
Hothy dismisses the Sztojay government, attempts armistice
with the Soviet Union.

October 1944
Germans arrest Horthy and install new Hungarian government
under fascist Arrow Cross Party leader Ferenc Szálasi.

November 1944
Budapest Jews march on foot to the Austrian border.

December 1944
Soviets surround Budapest; the Battle of Budapest begins.

December 1944
The Soviets set up a provisional government in Hungary, including representatives of several moderate parties.

January 1945
Hungary signs armistice.

February 1945
Soviets liberate Buda section of the city.

November 1945
The Independent Smallholders' Party wins free election but Soviets insist on a coalition government including the Communists, the Social Democrats and the National Peasant Party with Communists holding key government posts.

February 1946
Hungary declared a republic, leader of the Smallholders, Zoltán Tildy, becomes President, Ferenc Nagy becomes Prime Minister, Mátyás Rákosi, leader of the Communist Party, becomes Deputy Prime Minister.
Communist László Rajk becomes minister of the interior and establishes the Hungarian security police (ÁVH).

March 1945
Szálasi's government flee the country.

April 1945
Soviet troops drive the last German units and their Arrow Cross collaborators out of western Hungary.

February 1947
The Treaty of Peace with Hungary signed. Hungarian boundaries fixed as they existed on 1 January 1938 except for a minor loss of territory on the Czechoslovakian border. Ethnic Germans deported to Germany.

February 1947
Police begin arresting leaders of the Smallholders Party.

May 1947
Prominent figures emigrate or are forced into exile, including Prime Minister Ferenc Nagy.

August 1947
Communist Party commits election fraud with absentee ballots, but still fails to take majority and so abandons democratic façade.

June 1948
Social Democratic Party is forced to merge with the Communist Party to form the Hungarian Working People's Party. Árpád Szakasits given the role of President.

February 1949
All political parties forced into one 'People's Front' led by Rákosi. Opposition declared illegal.

August 1949
Country becomes the People's Republic of Hungary.

1949–56
Rákosi is de facto leader of Hungary with close ties to Russia.

May 1949
Minister of foreign affairs László Rajk arrested accused of spying and later executed. Within three years other leaders also arrested and imprisoned and Rákosi dictatorship begins.

February 1953
Stalin dies, Nikita Sergeyevich Khrushchev ascends, de-Stalinisation begins.

1953–55
Imre Nagy appointed as Chairman of the Council of Ministers (de facto Prime Minister) of the Hungarian People's Republic.

May 1955
Hungary joins the Warsaw Pact.

October 1956
Peaceful student demonstration in Budapest sets off a chain of events that leads to the Hungarian Revolution. Nagy becomes the leader of this rebellion against the Soviet-backed government, for which he is later hanged.

November 1956
Soviets send tanks and troops to quash uprising.

1956–88
Soviets install János Kádár as leader through the Socialist
Workers' Party; government gradually becomes less hard line.

1968
Free market elements enter Hungary's socialist economy.

1988
Kádár replaced by Károly Grósz. Opposition groups form the
Hungarian Democratic Forum.

1989
Kádár dies.

March 1989
Symbolic reburial of Imre Nagy takes place. Speakers call for
withdrawal of Soviet troops.

May 1989
Free elections held, Hungarian Democratic Forum elected.
József Antall becomes Prime Minister.

May 1989
Border with Austria opens, communist state in Hungary is
dismantled and a transition to a multi-party democracy starts.

1989
Fall of communism leads to the eventual break-up of the
Soviet Union, marking the end of the Cold War.

1990

A centre-right coalition wins elections; Hungary withdraws from Warsaw Pact military exercises.

1991

Soviet forces withdraw from Hungary; the Warsaw Pact is dissolved.

1999

Hungary joins NATO.

2004

Hungary joins EU, OECD, WTO and IMF.

2010

Conservative parliament comes to power with Prime Minister Viktor Orbán. He is re-elected for a fourth term in April 2022.

Notes

Introduction

1. www.worldjewishcongress.org/en/about/communities/HU
2. www.theguardian.com/world/2000/sep/19/1
3. Victor Sebestyen, *Twelve Days of Revolution 1956* (London: Phoenix, 2007), p.xxiii.

Epilogue

1. United States Holocaust Memorial Museum
   https://encyclopedia.ushmm.org/content/en/article/hungary-after-the-german-occupation
2. https://encyclopedia.ushmm.org/content/en/article/hungary-before-the-german-occupation
3. https://apnews.com/article/eaa56bb88684410d987da53d255c7367
4. www.wilsoncenter.org/blog-post/right-return-home-victims-gulag-are-waging-legal-battle-reparation

Acknowledgements

If this book shows anything, it is that it's the human connections we make that form our own life story. I consider it an enormous privilege that Marta chose to share her family's story with me, that she allowed me to ask all manner of questions and then trusted me to pour the results of our many conversations into this book. Examining original documents that are close to eighty years old, that have survived both a labour camp and a communist regime, and are the sort of thing that I would usually only get to peer at through a glass case, was an absolute honour.

Thank you Marta for allowing me to become part of this story's journey.

I would also like to thank Laura, for taking the first step in introducing me to Marta, to Tom for the initial help he gave me in how I could best mould this opportunity into a book and everyone at Pen & Sword for their help and support from manuscript to final product (I absolutely love the cover Paul Wilkinson!).

Thank you to Laura Marks OBE, inter-faith social activist and policy advisor, who has founded and chaired organisations including Mitzvah Day International and the Holocaust Memorial Day Trust. And also to the much-missed Vanessa Rosenthal (1943–2022), an actor and writer, whose autobiography *Inside Out (A Life in Stages)* documents her journey of reconciliation with her Jewish faith.

Disclaimer

Some names have been changed. The book contains Marta's historical recollections and may not be factually accurate.